MW00775172

The Fledgling Years

The Fledgling Years

William C. Macklon

Western Producer Prairie Books
Saskatoon, Saskatchewan

Cover illustration by Joanne Oldring Sydiaha
Untitled 1987, pencil on arches (detail)
Courtesy of ARTWORKS, Saskatoon

Cover design by Robert Grey

Printed and bound in Canada

The publisher acknowledges the support received for this publication from the Canada Council.

Western Producer Prairie Books is a unique publishing venture located in the middle of western Canada and owned by a group of prairie farmers who are members of Saskatchewan Wheat Pool. From the first book in 1954, a reprint of a serial originally carried in the weekly newspaper, *The Western Producer,* to the book before you now, the tradition of providing enjoyable and informative reading for all Canadians is continued.

Canadian Cataloguing in Publication Data

Macklon, William C. (William Charles), 1919–

    The fledgling years

    ISBN 0-88833-344-7

1. Macklon, William C. (William Charles), 1919–
2. Frontier and pioneer life – Saskatchewan.
I. Title.

FC3522.1.M33A3 1990   971.24'02'092   C90-097117-7
F1072.M33A3 1990

Contents

*To the prairie women
who did it all*

"So fair and foul a day
I have not seen"

I was born in December of 1919 in Kinley, Saskatchewan. That's in what
we call Western Canada, although there's a lot of Canada farther west
than that. I always thought I was born in the shack that still stands
there, and which my father bought for seventy-five dollars when he
first got work as a grain buyer for the State Elevator Company. The
company lent him the money against his pay and got it back at fifteen
dollars a month. The shack had two rooms at the time but my dad later
built a shed-roofed kitchen on the back so that it could accommodate
us all: older brother, Harold; two sisters, Ethel and Connie; me; and
a couple of years later, a younger brother, Walter. But Connie told me
not long ago that I was born in the Kinley Hotel. I suppose they must
have had a birthing room set up there because a lot of people lived
in crowded shanties like ours and there were certainly no hospitals within
reach. We were lucky that a doctor practiced in Perdue, the next village
down the line, and he must have come over when word somehow
reached him of an impending or, more likely, an already-over delivery.
The communities had telephone lines, but I don't know if they had long
distance capabilities.

But there is a story I was told about when the telephone first came
to Kinley. There was this fellow who was a great favorite of all, being
a hard worker as well as an all-round athlete. But he had the unfortunate

habit of using language, the kind that horrified preachers and gave delicate ladies the vapors. So the guys on his threshing gang got talking about the new telephone lines that were going into the farms round about and they persuaded their friend that people would be able to pick him up on their telephones. The poor boob hardly cussed more than a dozen or two times during the next few days until somebody took pity.

There's a story about that hotel, too. A few years ago when I was about sixty-seven, Dorothy and I were driving around the vicinity looking over what's left of my roots. We wanted to run down to see what they'd done to Pike Lake and it was getting late, so we booked a room at the hotel in Delisle before we left—quite nice by the way. Next day we drove over to Kinley where we got talking to the postmaster who'd also been born in Kinley, even before I was. I found out that the Kinley Hotel had been torn down and the lumber taken to Delisle and rebuilt there away back in the late twenties. Apparently, I had slept in my birthplace without knowing it.

How my family came to be in Kinley was more or less accidental. Dad's cousin, Will Smith, came to Canada from London about 1903 as a British veteran of the Boer War and took up a place on the shore of Last Mountain Lake. His nearest town was Strasbourg. I suppose that, among other things, he acted as scout for the rest of the Smith family and for my dad.

Will's letters home must have been persuasive because his brother Arthur, also a veteran, and my dad, nineteen years old, decided to join him in 1906. A few years later the Smith parents and two daughters, Helen and Ivy, followed.

I don't think either the Smiths or the Macklons lived much above the poverty line in England, and at that time, that was pretty far down, indeed, although there were plenty even worse off. The Smith lads had some help from the British government because of their war service, but my dad had only a bit of savings. He must have fancied joining his cousins in the great adventure because he signed a written contract with his uncle, Smith Senior, the Smith boys' father, who financed him. Essentially, my dad contracted to come to the "colony," take a homestead and prove it up, and then turn it over to Smith Senior. Smith Senior, on his part, was to pay my dad's passage to Saskatchewan, "in The Northwest Territories," pay his lodging with cousin Will until a homestead was obtained, and then pay wages at the going rate until the homestead was proven up and the title transferred. There was nothing written down to show what thought they gave to meeting the costs of machinery, horses, and the like, or about who would get any crops that were grown in the interim. I think they just assumed that all three boys would be living cheek by jowl and that Will's equipment would serve all, and I think that whatever was produced on the farm went to Smith Senior. Upon transfer of the title to Smith Senior, my dad was also to receive 160 pounds less the sum expended for his passage and train fares to Will's place. I guess that meant that they figured the land at one pound per acre.

What emotions and impressions came to Dad when he landed with Arthur in Halifax at 10:00 A.M. on March 15, 1906, he kept to himself. The postcard he mailed that day to his brother back in England said only: "Just arrived 10 am good voyage got box through alright, Dick." Whatever he may have felt, it didn't seem to be elation or zeal to get started on the great adventure.

Anyway, after a time, the three lads abandoned Will's homestead and moved to land near Lockwood and within a mile or so of each other. As far as I know, they never came to blows.

Will Smith went on to build a prosperous farm, and Arthur just enjoyed life. My dad got farm hand's wages for three years to keep him from starvation while he developed the homestead, and maybe three or four hundred dollars. Not much, but better than a cold handshake and a kick in the pants.

After that he took up a preemption, which was a sort of second homestead and married his cousin, Helen Smith. They used their combined threshing-crew wages to buy five horses in the fall, of which two got sick and died, and the rest were killed when they were turned out to forage for the winter and strayed onto the railway tracks. That ended any further notions of farming. They moved into a shack in Lockwood and Dad became somewhat of a jack-of-all-trades, working as a plasterer's helper, harvesting, and helping at one of the elevators. My brother Harold was born there and spent most of a day headfirst down a badger hole just outside the town before he was found and rescued. My sister Ethel came along, and as for Dad, he probably cursed the day he'd left his home and family in London. He must surely have expected never to see them again.

About the time World War One began, he wrote applications to all the grain elevator companies and was taken on as a helper at Kinley by the State Elevator Company. At first that was only steady work through the fall season, so he had to manage through the rest of the year with part-time jobs at the elevators, and anything he could find.

He wrote a letter to his brother Charles on June 30, 1915, mentioning his satisfaction that Charles had been able to move his family farther away from the bombed area near the London docks, where he worked. It's an interesting letter.

> I am working in the Garage now and am quite an expert on Fords and am getting pretty good on any make of car. I bought a Ford for Bill Smith, $450.00 a couple of weeks ago and he came up here on Sat. and we all drove down to Lockwood about 150 miles over prairie roads. We started about ½ past eight in the morning and got there about ½ past seven at night went through Saskatoon. We stopped on the road and had lunch which we took with us and also stopped in one town and had icecream and drinks. It was a fierce hot day but the little old Ford went jake, some little old bus, ain't they. There is one in the town next to us that has travelled over 150 thousand miles and is running every day carrying mail. Would not mind if I had one still I don't do so bad as I can mostly get a car at the garage if I want to go anywhere.

Of interest, too, were his comments about prices, wages, and wartime conscription.

> Of course I go back in the elevator this fall 15 Aug. and they have given me a raise $110.00 a month not so rotten but the living is ding-busted high say listen 35¢ a lb. strawberries. 35¢ each cucumbers. 40¢ lb. butter. 12½¢ qt. milk. 25¢ lb. sausages. We buy flour and make our own bread if bought 12½¢ a loaf which the boy could eat in one meal.

and

> We have conscription here now and they are taking everyone (that is single) between 20 and 25 even off the farm so maybe you will see me over there one of these days.

My parents spent ten or twelve years in Kinley and brought three more children into the world, and my dad got his Model T. I started school there at Easter of 1925 when I was five years old, and then, in July, Dad was hired as one of their first five agents by the new Saskatchewan Wheat Pool, and we moved away. But we still drove back to Kinley several times a year to visit friends, to attend the fair or ball tournament, and for my dad to play cricket, which remained a popular sport at Kinley until about 1930. So there are lots of stories from Kinley that I remember experiencing or hearing about – or that possibly I just imagine – but the memories are a jumble of unrelated things.

A jumble
of unrelated things

There were lots of fads. Most of them were innocent enough. Dining room tables were taken out of service for weeks by gigantic unfinished jigsaw puzzles or by completed ones left intact to bully and amaze any callers. Bridge parties became twice-weekly affairs and hot arguments raged everywhere over Contract and Auction. But there were evil fads too. Hair was first bobbed and then shingled, and soon curling irons heated in the chimneys of kerosene lamps imposed sinful marcels upon hair that had once been chaste and straight as God intended. Dress hems rose indecently, rolled-down hose soon followed, and flappers with painted cheeks even rouged their peek-a-boo knees. Worse still, some daring girls – but no ladies – lapsed into the secret application of lipstick.

One morning my mother took me and my baby brother to call on a neighbor lady. Mum carried my brother but I was old enough to follow behind, stepping along one rut of the buggy-trail street. Mum rapped on the wood of the storm door which hadn't yet been taken down to be replaced by the screen door for summer. No one came. It seemed strange. She rapped a few more times and took a peek through the kitchen window. Nobody there. I don't know why the urgency, maybe she thought the lady had suffered a swooning as ladies used to do. Anyway, she went round and took a peek through the lace curtains of the front room. I heard a shriek and then after a few minutes the lady appeared at her door in blushing confusion. She'd been hiding under the table—she'd bobbed her hair.

Another fad, I suppose you could call it, but it must have been only for the well-to-do farm people, was the ownership of a Shetland pony and trap. Someone south of town near the Eagle Creek bridge on the correction line raised the ponies. At one time he must have had a hundred or more—Shetlands and Welsh. It was a great thrill trying to count them all as we drove by in my dad's Model T. But the traps thrilled me even more. I remember only once having a ride in one. Two schoolgirl friends of my sister Connie picked her and me up as we were walking along the sandy north road near the first wooden bridge. We each carried bunches of buffalo beans and tiger lilies which made it hard to climb up through the little door at the back, but once seated, two facing two, I was ecstatic. We bowled along with the little paint pony trotting happily beneath us and farting zestfully now and again, making the girls peek at each other and blush.

The traps were made by Mr. Woods, the blacksmith. He must have learned his trade in England for there were no other traps like his and he made them almost entirely by hand because there was no electricity, except way off thirty miles away in the big city.

Before I started school I spent many hours silently watching him. But now and again I would have to go off for a bit when he started up the big engine. Its huge flywheels churning relentlessly around sent wide leather belts swishing up into the dark, their laces blip, blip, blipping against the jackshaft pulleys. If I stayed I'd be terrified when Mr. Woods pulled a lever to start the terrible pounding of his trip hammer or a stream of fire from the big grinding wheel.

But I came back because as soon as the engine died I knew that the magic would begin again: the flimsy hacksaw blade would melt through strap-iron, the wooden folding rule would straighten, marks would be punched, and the post drill would twist out silvery coils of steel leaving perfect holes precisely spaced and countersunk for screws and bolts. Then, after the last screw was driven home and the last nut turned down against its washer, a few remaining sharp corners were smoothed away and the fresh smell of paint filled the shop while Mr. Woods applied brown and green and red, with delicate yellow stripes and filigrees to complete each masterpiece.

Another memory of Kinley is of wearing a pair of my sister's cast-off shoes. They were high shoes that came up above the ankle and had to be buttoned up the sides with a button hook. Everyone had lots of button hooks because whenever the ladies sent off to Eaton's catalogue for a pair of shoes they came in the mail complete with a new button hook. When it came time for me to go to my first day at school though, I had proper lace-up boots, and my mum sat me up on the kitchen table and taught me how to lace them and tie a bow. I wore short pants that she'd sewn up out of an old pair of my dad's and which were held up by suspenders. I was only just five so she also gave me a lesson in managing suspenders and buttons just in case I had to visit the school privy.

It's funny, but the only thing that remains of that first school experience is that one day the teacher asked if any of us could say a rhyme. Only one of us could, but in the end he was too overcome with shyness to say it out loud. The teacher, ever resourceful, persuaded him that it would be alright if he just whispered it into her ear. Here's what he whispered:

> There is a happy land far far away
> Where little piggies stand, bright, bright as day.
> Boy! You should see them run
> When they see the butcher come.
> Three slices off their bum
> Three times a day.

Now, where in the world could he have learned a verse like that!

Cigareets and
whuskey and wild, wild women

If you wanted to be a man you learned to smoke at an early age. It wasn't easy to become an addict of the weed because we had no money. Still most of us managed it by the time we were twelve. Only fast girls would smoke and we were too keen on the sins of tobacco use to notice if any of the girls were fast.

Most of the tobacco was "swiped" so we took whatever we could get, and we tried other things as well – rolled-up newspaper or cornsilk. It was even rumored that down in the school barn some of the boys had resorted to dried horse manure and had found it not bad. In my own case I realize that I must have been somewhat backward because I can remember using only O.P. (other people's), except once, when I was six, I swiped some makings from my dad but didn't know how to roll 'em.

My first smoke was with Mr. Woods's boy at Kinley. He'd found a cigar some place and we went over to the tracks and walked east until we came to a big culvert. There was no water in it so we hid in there. One of us had swiped a handful of kitchen matches. That was easy to do because everybody had a match dispenser hanging near the stove for lighting fires and coal-oil lamps. The dispensers usually had advertising on them from the store that gave them out for Christmas and they held a full box of wooden lucifers. For some reason my friend cut the cigar in two lengthwise, so I don't think our smoke could have been all that successful. Nevertheless, we drank a lot of water from somebody's pump on the way home and examined each other for the telltale signs of "singed eyelashes" before daring to appear back in society. I remember that my mum was peeling apples when I came in so I grabbed a handful of peels and chewed them down in case any smell still lingered. I was five.

That summer my dad packed up all our stuff and moved it with a team and hayrack to Birdview. That was its name then, but they changed it to Donavon because all its mail kept being sent to Broadview. The move was hard on my older brother, Harold, because there was no school in Birdview so, at fourteen, he had to drive us in my dad's Model T to a one-roomed school called Norquay School two and a half miles out in the country. In Kinley he'd got into the habit of playing hooky from school and going rabbit hunting along Eagle Creek with another bad boy, often in the "borrowed" car of the boy's father. One day Harold's pal drove his dad's car through the back wall of the garage so that ended the "borrowing." Together they had also smoked a good many cigarettes. He had to give that up too when he drove us in the Ford. It was just as well, the guilt was getting to him.

He told me once, later, that he'd been down on the main street in Kinley one Saturday and had seen a man wearing some kind of uniform go into the general store. It scared him. He slipped into the poolroom and asked Jack who that guy was. Jack was aware of my brother's sins so he told him it was a policeman looking for kids who were smoking cigarettes. My brother hightailed it the mile or so up to North Kinley on the CPR line where he hid under the driveway of an elevator until it got dark. He figured later that the policeman must have been a Salvation Army guy collecting donations.

Our family left Donavon after a year and moved to Laura, using the same modes of transport—hayrack and Model T. All the boys there smoked, too, when they could get it, and never refused chewing tobacco or snoose if they were offered. At Laura they had a two-roomed elementary school and a separate high school, so the kids came in to town for school instead of leaving it as in Donavon. We lived just a skip and a hop from school, but the farm kids flocked into town every school day riding horses or driving buggies and democrats. So the school barn, besides sheltering the horses, provided a smoking retreat and once it was too cold for softball, not one boy would be visible in the school grounds at recess; they were all in the barn – an excellent location for those connoisseurs of horse manure.

One afternoon after recess we were going to practice singing "Dem Golden Slippers" in blackface for the Christmas concert, and we came back from the barn stinking to high heaven. Teacher got us boys all lined up ready to go when suddenly her nose twitched and her face went angry. She went along the row sniffing us with disgust. At the middle she came upon Wilbert, going on for six foot and stalled in the fifth grade. "Wilbert," she demanded, "does your mother know you smoke?"

Wilbert's voice had to choose that moment to escape its newly acquired masculine depth. "No," he squeaked, "but she knows I chew."

"Dem Golden Slippers" got laid away that day. We all had to write out "I will not smoke cigarettes" one hundred times. Some of us had to stay in to get finished. Well, one thing, we all learned how to spell "cigarettes." Some of us also learned how to write two lines at once using two pencils gripped between the fingers of the writing hand – probably a first in the development of the duplicator. As for Wilbert, I believe he went on to become a millionaire farmer and a good one at that. And I did hear that he served as chairman of his local school board until the school was closed down in favor of busing.

Fortunately, booze was scarce. I believe pretty well all the adults, either out of inclination or of necessity, were nominally teetotal. There were no bars or saloons or what we euphemistically call "licenced premises"; that may have accounted for most of the abstinence because there did come a time just after prohibition ended when making homemade beer became a semisecret vice and the product of it used to be inflicted upon all visitors. Many a ceiling received an out-of-season repaint because yesterday a careless host had opened an explosively overcharged bottle.

My dad usually brought back a part bottle of scotch when he returned from his annual week at the big city bonspiel, and it was kept on the cellar steps for medicinal purposes. One hot summer day, nobody was around, so I took a big jolt out of it just to see what it would do. I managed not to drop the bottle, but I gave up breathing for about eight minutes and enough tears rolled down my face to soak the front of my shirt.

One spring, the town boys decided to do something about the waste of all the perfectly good dandelions that grew everywhere. Dandelion wine, we'd heard, was even better than chokecherry. A few of us managed to swipe enough sugar to make about five pounds. It wasn't all that difficult because people bought their sugar by the hundredweight, it being always needed for canning saskatoons or something, and the sacks could be used for dishtowels after. Our knowledge of the fermentation process was so faulty that after we'd mixed it all up, we bottled it right off and hid it in an abandoned woodshed. In the morning all the corks had blown so we whittled some up out of poplar wood and drove them in with a hammer. Most of the bottles shattered inside a day or two, but a couple survived and we met in the evening to have a good drunk-up, thinking to sneak home to bed after, and no one the wiser.

Well, it turned out to be us who were the wiser. The damn stuff was fizzy and sweet, but except for a bit of a tickly nose, it produced no titillation at all, let alone the drunken orgy we had hoped to enjoy.

We had no need of sex education. We learned all there was to know through a combination of listening to pubescent elders and itinerant hired men, observing the behaviour of animals, and checking out the corset pages in the mail order catalogues. By seven most of us had it down pretty well as it eventually turned out to be, barring a few minor exceptions.

My first lesson in the ways of women came when we moved to Frontenac School while I was still in grade one and I found myself sitting in a double desk with a GIRL. We used to have these cards with a picture outlined in holes punched through. They were called sewing cards and were given to little kids to amuse them while the older ones had their lessons. You had a blunt needle and some colored cord to sew in and out the holes, and if you did it right, you ended up with a picture of a cat or a duck outlined in red or purple cord.

You also had a pair of blunt scissors for cutting the cord. So this GIRL dared me to cut a hole in her long, cotton knit stocking, and then she went and "told" when I took her up on it. Mr. Hartridge put his foot up on my seat and sprawled me over his knee while he spanked me. Then he made me sew up the hole with the stocking still on her leg, using brown sewing card cord.

These days there's a lot of talk about teen-age sex but nothing much is said about love, so I don't know if kids fall in love any more or not. In my own case, I was always in love, and pretty constant about it at that. My trouble, which bothered me considerably whenever I had nothing else to do, was that the girl never seemed to be in love with me. Worse, she was always acting as if she had just fallen in love with someone else, although when I look back, it seems possible that she might not have acted that way if she hadn't noticed me looking.

Anyway, boys, from an early age, were all in love. The trouble was, in these small communities, there were very few eligible girls. Oh, sure, there were about as many girls as boys, but there was only one or maybe three that were loveable. The rest were tattletales and dingbats as far as we boys were concerned. So that meant that almost all of us ended up in love with the same girl, and it really ruined her. That girl became so conceited that I'm pretty sure she could never get over it; she'd have to spend the rest of her life unable to find anyone sufficiently exalted to associate with.

The other girls, though, didn't seem to be affected. They seemed to be altogether unaware of our astute observations. They just went on playing dolls, chording "doctor, doctor, come here quick" on the school piano at recess, passing autograph albums back and forth, and giggling a lot. And another thing they'd do was to sit facing each other and play a hand-clapping game to the tune of "There Oughtta Be A Moonlight Saving Time," and going on and on faster and faster until one of them miscued. Then they'd start all over again. It was insane!

On Sundays in the summer my family usually went off to Kinley in the Model T to visit or to picnic and swim along Eagle Creek, but once it got wintry and the roads closed in, the routine changed. After morning Sunday School we kids went home to big Sunday dinners, and then parents would find comfortable chairs to snooze in while their food digested to music from their battery-powered radios. So we'd wander around town until we'd gathered up six or seven boys and girls and we'd walk east out the tracks as far as the coulee, or west to the first or second crossing, depending on the mood of the girls. With the right girls it seemed a pretty exciting pastime. In fact, some of the older blades even bragged once that they'd gone a lot farther than that with some of the girls – all the way to Tessier and back.

Is there
a doctor in the house?

There was a movie house in Perdue from an early date. My dad
sometimes took us there from Kinley in the Model T, and if anyone
had actually called for a doctor during the show, he just might have
been found in the audience. But, generally, there were no doctors, and
if there was one, his activity was pretty well limited to inflicting unjust,
painful, and expensive ordeals upon people too sick or ignorant to object.

There was a doctor involved at some stage in my birth, but I was
six years old before one again laid hands on me. I was lucky that I was
too young for the big Kinley tonsillectomy carnival.

Somehow the bright idea came about that tonsils were a bit of foreign
matter in the throat that, if left in place, would have consequences so
dire they didn't bear thinking about. Best get 'em out before they could
begin their devilish work, and the sooner the better. So they organized
a working bee one Saturday at the school. They brought the doc over
from Perdue, someone who'd once been a nurse assisted, and a few
of the women volunteered as clean-up staff. The bewildered parents
from miles around arrived according to schedule, dragging their petrified
children, and they ran the whole kaboodle of school kids through the
operation using the two teachers' desks pulled together for an operating
table. My older brother and, I think, my two sisters went through it
so I guess they must have "tonsillectomized" twenty or thirty victims

that day, maybe more. So far as I know they all lived.

My own first encounter with a health matter came when I was found to be infested with cooties (head lice). All us kids had them. My mum believed that we caught them at school and I remember that she figured she could name who gave them to us. I doubt if she was right, though, because after we exterminated the little beggars we never got them again, although we continued to sit and play with the suspected carriers. I remember that my mum got the fine-tooth comb and combed us out over a sheet of newspaper, and then she folded the bugs into the middle and threw it into the cookstove fire. Everybody seems to have had fine-tooth combs about the house in the twenties. I suspect they were another of the little premiums sent out by the mail order houses along with the parcels of merchandise. And, apparently, nobody was offended to get one, any more than they were by a button hook, a shoe horn, a paper of pins, or by a card of hooks and eyes, snap fasteners, or rick rack braid.

Every night the cooties rained onto the paper, but their numbers never seemed to decrease. After a few days all the kids in town must have been harboring a thriving population of them, so that the mums finally had to overcome their mortification and consult each other until somebody came up with a cure—kerosene or, as we called it then, coal oil.

The way my mum used it was to pour a goodly dollop onto our crowns and work it in until both hair and scalp were saturated. Then she wrapped our little noggins in towels and put us to bed. Luckily it was Friday night because the next morning we woke up early with scalps redder than spanked bums and three times as painful. But it killed the lice, and Monday morning we were able to keep up our good attendance records even though we spent the rest of the week peeling.

The smallpox vaccination marathon held in Laura when I was about six traumatized a lot of us school kids, but nobody paid any attention so we just had to get over it by ourselves. Actually I don't think the word "trauma" had even been invented, so people thought it appropriate, and certainly very efficient, to use the schools as convenient sites for inflicting torture upon children.

The first warning of impending pain came when I arrived at school to see a Model T parked next to the back door. Most of the other kids were already there, and in the boys' cloakroom a stunned-looking audience was gathered around one of the big farm lads who had mounted the janitor's stepladder. He was telling in terrifying detail the sadistic injury and excruciating pain that we were about to suffer at the hands of Ol' Doc Cameron. He described syringes injecting gallons of medicine through oversized needles shoved into our puny arms. The arms, he said, would swell like inflated inner tubes, and three days later would come up in a huge and dangerous scab which, if it got knocked off, might be the death of us. Any doubts we might have harbored were quickly removed when time arrived for the bell to be rung and nothing happened; when some incautious youngster attempted to open the classroom door it was locked, something hitherto unheard of.

When those in charge finally felt we had been sufficiently terrified, we heard the key rattle inside, sounding like the summons of a jailor unlocking the death cell door before leading a blubbering convict along that last, long walk to the gallows. After a pause the door opened enough to let a teacher squeeze through to confirm that we were going to be vaccinated, starting with the Grade Ones first and ending up with the older kids from the high school who would be coming over in the afternoon. There was nothing to be afraid of, she said, we'd hardly feel a thing. Hah! Who did she think we were?

I can't remember what we did all day except stand in groups of one, paralyzed with fear and imagining every conceivable and inconceivable torture that awaited us. I don't think we were allowed to go home, not even us townies, for I remember the big girls going in long after my own ordeal was over and returning to titillate us with the information that they had been done on their thighs, where the scar wouldn't show. All in all there were a lot of tears, not a few screams, and even some faintings. But for a few days after, most of us were able to regain status by bragging about the size of our swollen limbs or by warning classmates about the perils of knocking loose the huge scabs that formed as the swelling receded. It was some compensation. But it was tough beans for the ones whose vaccination didn't "take."

A couple of year later, though, when diphtheria inoculations came out, someone decided we should be done on a Saturday in the Grain Growers' Hall. Again there was a high sense of panic in the crowded building, but there were plenty of strong men ready to pinion and subdue any kickers and screamers. However most of us could at least pretend a blasé indifference, having come through the big vaccination marathon without any noticeable permanent injury except for a few tics and stutters and the odd recurring nightmare.

About the only other medical attention anyone was likely to be driven to seek was a session in Doc Cameron's tooth-pulling chair in Delisle.

Doc was one of several doctors around the province who pulled teeth, but he was one of the few who used novocaine if you wanted it. It didn't always work, though.

Doc Cameron also owned a farm where he raised silver foxes, but he always made time for doctoring, and especially to visit another medical marvel upon us. That was quarantine. Quarantine was a sort of jail sentence passed on you in retaliation for getting certain diseases. The doc tacked a cardboard placard to your door and nobody was supposed to go in or out until the disease had run its course through every member of the household. In the case of a big family with anything serious that might take all winter. Once the last patient had either recovered or succumbed, the survivors were evacuated and sulphur candles were ignited in every room from cellar to attic and left to burn behind sealed doors. Some hours or even days later, when it was thought the place was sufficiently "fumigated," doors and windows were flung open to let fresh air blow out most of the fumes, and the family's surviving members crept back into their home to lie low for another six months or so until the scandal was forgiven if not forgotten. At least it was hell on bedbugs.

It was scarlet fever that brought quarantine to the people of Laura. It started in the fall with one of the larger families, and the frogs were singing springtime mating calls in McCurdy's Slough before the family was able to emerge back into the social round.

The other families, more afraid of the crimson placard than of the disease, withdrew from the community. The bonspiel nearly had to be postponed. Dances were sparsely attended, and at the midnight break, the dancers were afraid to eat the sandwiches and cake provided by the ladies, and which normally would have disappeared before the first cup of coffee had been dipped from the washboiler on the big Quebec heater at the back by the door. Some even missed the Christmas concert, which wasn't all that great anyway because it was missing some of its best performers.

At the general store sales went up on Crisco, Ipana toothpaste, and Maxwell House coffee because we spent so many nights huddled near the radio listening to Fred Allen, Jack Benny, and Amos 'n Andy, so we caught all the commercials. Most of us had to hunger unappeased for the bliss that inhaling the smoke of a Lucky or a Chesterfield could have brought if only we had been born on the right side of the line where you could buy a whole carton for a mere buck-fifty.

At school, we students broke up into little cliques which spent recess covertly watching each other for "peelers," because you never could tell who might be concealing a fevered relative at home, hoping to elude Doc Cameron and his quarantine placard. It was well known that peeling skin was a sure sign of the scarlet plague. And sure enough it wasn't long after the post-Christmas-concert boredom set in that somebody spotted a peeler and tattled to the teacher. Poor old Doc Cameron had to get out his Model T with the Sears-Roebuck bogey wheels and caterpillar tread and drive it, side curtains flapping, about nine miles down the railway tracks only to find nothing more malignant than a picked-at wart. All the same, he did some good, because he threatened the next idiot who called him out on a fool's errand with a bill in the mail. And, besides, our former fascination with adolescent cliques gave way to excited discussions of the marvellous, incredible, futuristic sight of the doc's Model T bouncing along the railway line with a blizzard of snow flying behind its churning tracks.

So for the most part doctoring was a domestic art practiced by mothers, and every kitchen cupboard had a medicine shelf where she kept her favorite remedies. What she kept depended largely on the ethnic makeup of the family. My mother kept jars of goose grease which was used as a chest rub for lung congestion. Flaxseed was good for constipation, and if a seed was put into the eye, it would collect any dust or grit so that could be easily removed with the seed. A teaspoonful of camphor oil heated over the coal-oil lamp could be poured into an aching ear, and a boil could be brought to a head by a poultice made with bread softened with boiling water and a few drops of vinegar. Burns were smeared with petroleum jelly.

Kinley had kind of sandy soil and so my dad had driven down a sand point in the kitchen and screwed a green-painted cistern pump onto the pipe so we had pretty good water right there in the house. One morning my older sister, Ethel, wanted to brush her teeth, so she poured half a cup of boiling water from the kettle and brought it over to the pump to add some cold. When she raised the pump handle she knocked over the cup and the boiling water splashed all over my little brother Walter's shoulder. Because it soaked his clothes, it had scalded him pretty badly by the time anyone thought to undress him. We called a neighbor lady who had been a nurse and she treated him for a week or more by dressing the scalds with cloth smeared with Vaseline, which she baked in the oven and cooled before she applied them. Although the treatment left my brother with big, ugly scars on his arm and down his side, it did heal up without getting infected, so my mum was very grateful for the help.

My sister must have been going through a disastrous stage where the wise would have avoided her. One spring day we kids were out back by the woodpile where Ethel was having fun chopping the axe into the big chopping block and then prying it loose. I came along with a large pigweed I'd pulled, and it seemed like a good idea to put the end of the weed on the block for my sister to chop. Since she seemed to be agreeable, I fed the weed in an inch or so every time the axe came up. The trouble was that she didn't stop when I ran out of weed and so I went bawling into the house with a big gash in the back of my five-year-old hand. We had a visitor who grabbed a bottle and poured the contents over my wound, but what he thought was hydrogen peroxide turned out to be carbolic acid which was there for disinfecting the slop bucket. The carbolic raised a big blister where it ran over my hand, but it all healed up pretty well although I still have the scars of the axe and the carbolic burn.

It quite amazes me that we never seemed to worry about or suffer infections. Nobody had tetanus shots and there were no antibiotics. Furthermore, bleeding wounds were sometimes stanched with a mud pack made by urinating into the dust. It was common for kids who mostly went barefoot once the snow was off the ground to cut their feet on broken glass, or worse still, to step on a rusty nail sticking out of a discarded board.

A favorite subject for the calendar art of the day was a boy dressed in a bib overall and a ragged straw hat, and with a big bandanna handkerchief wrapped around a sore big toe. But, in fact, it was no joke. I once ran on to a three-inch nail sticking up through a piece of shiplap lumber that someone had chucked away in a weedy patch. It went through the sole of my running shoe and almost through my foot so that I couldn't get my shoe off until I could draw the nail. But when I pulled on it, it seemed to pinch the flesh into the hole in the rubber. I had to sit down for about ten minutes twisting the board back and forth until the nail finally came out far enough that I could take out the shoelace and lift my foot free. Even then there was a half-inch of nail still sticking through the rubber sole. My foot swelled up hot and red and big as an apple, but in three or four days I was mobile again.

We never went in much for patent medicines, probably because they were too expensive. But many a woman came through the anxiety and exhaustion of pioneer life thanks only to frequent doses of "nerve food" or of "Lydia E. Pinkham's Vegetable Compound." Certain kidney pills were thought to relieve backaches, and they must have worked because they sure made you pee red for a few days. Purifying the blood was believed to be frequently required, especially after a long winter indoors. This was easily accomplished by taking some herbal brew, although there were a lot of concoctions with fancy names which cost a lot more and were really only mixtures of some or all of the known laxatives. For real pain there were three or four products containing opium available at any general store, and if you were old and full of aches and rheumatism, there was "Doctor Forney's Alpenkrauter," one of a group of remedies with a good shot of pure grain alcohol in every dose.

The halcyon days

We moved out of Donavon at Christmas time because the house we'd rented was needed by its owner. As there was no other accommodation in town my dad found a big farmhouse four miles out. It was a big change for me, and that place came to contribute some of the most vivid recollections of my life.

We had to change schools for a start and our teacher was a lad of about eighteen who brought an innovative approach to classroom management, to say the least.

The school was a typical one-roomed affair except that it had a raised platform across the front which Mr. Hartridge used as an extended pitcher's mound. One minute he would appear to be writing away, putting some assignment on the blackboard, and then he would slyly break off a bit from the end of his chalk and suddenly wheel round and fire it at the head of some daydreamer or goof-off. Usually his aim was bang on and the lump that rose on the offender's noggin restored a compliant diligence that could last for hours. But he accidentally caught me on the forehead once when I raised my head just as the kid behind me was folding a paper hat out of a page torn from his scribbler, so I know about the lumps. And it made me especially appreciative of the drama that followed a few days later.

As with all such schools, Frontenac had its big, good-natured farm lad who, having long ago given up trying to cope with the mysteries of long division and King John's Magna Carta, had gravitated through various seatings (always toward the back) until he found a fairly comfortable spot in the rear next to the right-hand wall. There he could usually endure the boring routine, simulating stupidity in order to be left alone, and able to get away with an occasional stare out the windows on the opposite wall.

Then one afternoon when everyone was half-asleep and trying their best to look otherwise, Mr. Hartridge let go a zinger that bounced off the boy's skull and went flying into the corner. We heard the clatter of furniture as the boy sprang up and we all turned in horror expecting to see him barging his way to the front intent on giving teacher the hiding of his life.

But for once the teacher had to overlook our laughter because a grin even crossed his own face when the boy stood, shoulders back and belly out, like Jimmy Gardiner spellbinding an audience of good Liberal farmers, and yelled, "Chalk against chalk!" And then he sat back down and went on with the business of looking diligent.

Another of Hartridge's disciplinary measures was to make any cut-up continue his misdemeanor through the rest of the period. One boy had to stand up front with his eyes crossed for an hour or so. Hartridge always carried the school strap in the side pocket of his jacket, but one evening he accepted an invitation to supper at the house of one school family where everyone hung their coats in the kitchen porch, and one of the boys swiped the strap and buried it out behind the barn. Hartridge never pursued the matter, but he got hold of an eighteen-inch chunk of one-inch rubber hose and found he could manage just as well with that.

There were many marvellous things in that school. There was a globe representing the earth that was mounted at its correct angle in a metal halo and it was fastened to a long cord that passed over a pulley at the ceiling. The cord was tied to a coat hook on the wall so that the globe floated up in space just like a real world. Teacher must have lowered it one day and given a lesson to another grade, and I must have neglected the story of "The Little Red Hen" in *The Canadian Reader* to kibitz, because that year I understood why the world turned on its axis and the consequence of the axis standing at a slant.

Another marvel was the supply box. It was a big, homemade wooden trunk with a padlock that was built against the wall farthest from the windows. In this school we were supplied with all our notebooks, pencils, pen nibs, and ink powder by the taxpayers. These were ordered from Eaton's catalogue every summer and went into the box to start each new year. A glimpse into the fabulous richness it contained was breathtaking.

I don't remember how I was taught to read, although I do remember when I was in grade three watching a teacher tell a new beginner that "cuh – aa – tuh" was "cat." But I must have been a dab hand at it for I can still remember most of "The Little Red Hen" by heart because I liked it so much that I read it over and over, and that I read "The Sun and The North Wind" only once because I found it scary, although I had to read it for the teacher. Another one I liked was "The Gingerbread Man" although it was also a bit scary. But that was in grade two.

Of all the lessons that must have been taught by Mr. Hartridge, the only one I remember was to the beginners' class who started, as I had the previous year, right after the Easter holidays. The teacher lined up these five or six little kids to teach them the alphabet. He made it into a sort of relay, with the child at the head of the line shouting "ay" and then running around to the back of the line, whereupon the next child shouted "bee" and followed suit. There was one beautiful little boy among the group who had curly, black hair and a trusting, angelic face set off by shining, deep black eyes. The second time he reached the head of the line, I waited for him to call "ell," but he just stood there looking innocently up into the expectant face of authority. Then he loudly declared, "I don't like playing this game!"

Appropriately, his name was Daniel – Daniel Climenhega. After serving overseas in the war, Daniel earned a Beaver Club scholarship at the University of Saskatchewan and went on to the prestigious London School of Economics. Then he joined the United Nations, working in many strange and troubled lands. Sadly, he was struck by a car and killed on a street in Nairobi in 1969.

There were several other Climenhegas attending Frontenac School, and some of them still live and farm near there. John, who was two or three grades ahead of me, also went to the University of Saskatchewan, studying math and physics and he ended up as Dean of the Faculty of Arts and Science at the University of Victoria. There his interest in the field of astronomy won honors culminating in his having a minor planet named for him. Frontenac School and Mr. Hartridge deserve some credit.

In the winter Mr. Hartridge made us all hot cocoa to wash down our sandwiches. And he wasn't as mean as the teacher where we went to school in the Model T. She wouldn't let us bring our lunches in from the porch until noon, so they were always frozen. And sometimes she wouldn't let you go to the toilet when you were nearly busting. Mr. Hartridge never did that.

It was a practice at Frontenac School to have Nature Study after recess on Friday afternoons, and we kids were allowed to bring in things and creatures to study. One kid brought in a weasel in an egg crate with a piece of glass over the top to keep him in. But it didn't. Just after noon this fierce little animal pushed free past the glass and went tearing up and down the aisles with half the boys in pursuit and all the girls standing up on their seats, screaming in terror.

Another time a kid brought in an eagle and two of the big boys held it up by the wingtips so we could all see the span of them. Owls and hawks were considered to be chicken killers, so farmers shot them and hung them up on the fences in the belief they would scare others away. Some farm wives kept two or three guinea fowl with their chickens because they always spotted hawks and set up a terrible squawking.

There were many more birds, and a lot more kinds of birds, around in those days. And there were bumblebees everywhere, and millions of flowers. It's hard to believe how it was. I heard of hunters who accidentally fired off both barrels of their gun while trying to pack sand into a gopher hole and almost got killed by the shower of mallards that came raining down. I don't believe that really happened, but it could have – the ducks were thick enough and the hunters were dumb enough. One spring at Laura when I was seven or eight, I knew where to find over a hundred ducks' nests and I used to make the rounds and visit them nearly every day. Before they could hatch we had a big, cold, three-day rainstorm and the nests were all abandoned. I tried to incubate some of the eggs under a couple of my mum's chickens, but they'd got too cold, I guess.

And flowers! Kids picked thousands of them and pressed them in schoolbooks to be pasted into homemade booklets with construction paper covers. Once my dad took us in the Model T to pick saskatoons at Pike Lake. On the way we had a flat so he pulled off the road to fix it beside a big virgin prairie pasture. The pasture was completely red with prairie lilies and we kids jumped out and ran into them, whipping the heads off with sticks in our exhilaration, and finally returned, arms full of them, only to chuck them out along the road on the way home because we'd found yellow water lilies in the lake and thought them nicer.

And if you found a garden with sunflowers they were always crawling with big, fat, yellow-striped bumblebees. We used to catch them in a bottle and bring them home, but they died before we could ever figure out how to get them making honey.

The six months with Mr. Hartridge at Frontenac School saw me through the rest of grade one. By summer my dad had got moved to Laura, which was better because it had a company house and also because it was the most important town between Saskatoon and Kindersley, being the only one built on both sides of the tracks.

Nature calling

No one that I knew of had a bathroom or piped water or a sanitary disposal system. That didn't bother us. Water was carried in, two buckets at a time, from the nearest pump. And the slop bucket could be dumped down the privy pit or, more likely, just chucked out back of the house somewhere because the water would soon soak away in the dry, prairie soil and the family flock of poultry, together with the odd stray dog, would clean up the peelings and table scraps. An occasional can of Gillette's Lye sprinkled into the toilet pit kept the smell bearable if you had a strong constitution. It also stretched out its useable term before a fresh pit would need to be excavated and the building levered up onto a couple of round fence posts and rolled over the new site. Once the privy was relocated, the soil from the new pit was thrown into the old and mounded up, and it soon grew over with weeds.

Most little kids used a chamber pot for their after-dark calls but for older kids a trip out back after dark could be a frightening experience. There was nothing real, but a good deal imagined, that might get you as you sat all alone with no light because you had to shut off the flashlight to save the batteries. Fortunately we were distracted to a great degree by the need to keep alert to the likely presence of a flittering flashlight fairy. These mischievous sprites came out at dusk to lurk about privies, waiting for some witless user to lay a flashlight on the wooden seat where it took only the softest waft of the fairy's breath to send it rolling toward the hole and down into the pit. When I think of archaeologists excavating the latrines of Roman ruins to discover what Romans ate and what dropped out of their trouser pockets, it makes me wonder what will be thought of the hundreds of thousands of flashlights to be uncovered a thousand years hence. The loss of flashlights in some households became so devastating that men resorted to manufacturing a wire loop capable of snaring them and restoring them to service. It was even rumored that at least one parent became so mentally unhinged by the sadistic mischief of the fairies that he held a heedless child upside down by the heels while a flashlight was retrieved.

But for me nature called in a more proper way and with almost as much urgency. It must have begun on that farmstead outside of Donavon. There was a big, square house of the type a few pioneers were able to build when their early farming success persuaded them that their dynasty had begun. What tragedy had led to its abandonment I never knew, but it had a mysterious atmosphere about it which was scary, and fascinating, all at once. A long shelter of mature trees shut the yard away from the view of anyone passing by on the road, and besides the house and a garden patch, there were a number of the usual farm outbuildings together with a pig run and a small paddock. The three other boundaries were cultivated fields.

The house was of considerable grandeur. It had fourteen rooms on two floors, and it boasted glassed French doors into the big living room, stained-glass lights above the doors and windows, a full basement with a furnace, and, up on the roof, a widow's walk. The basement also had a well with a pipe up to the kitchen pump. Our few sticks of furniture could not begin to fill all that, so we lived on the ground floor through the remainder of that winter and heated our bit of living space with the new kitchen coal-and-wood range, which came from Eaton's catalogue at thirty-five dollars, and with a round Quebec heater that we'd brought along. These were banked up and dampened before bedtime and fought a losing battle against the cold before surrendering completely about three in the morning. Then at six my dad would get up and shake down the ashes, throw on coal, and open up the drafts and dampers to get the place warm for the rest of us still in our beds.

I'd had whooping cough about the time we moved there so I remember little of the winter except of slogging the quarter mile or so through deep snow to attend Frontenac School. But I remember Saturday nights when my dad always brought home the weekend edition of *The Chicago Herald* with its color comics for us kids.

Those comics afforded us kids many hours of play time. First of all, my older sister would sit at the kitchen table and read them out loud as we crowded around trying to follow the action from panel to panel. Then the girls would take "Tillie The Toiler" and other favorites and cut out the figures along with the various clothes and fashion accessories that were printed with tabs to fold back so they could be hung on the cartoon people. The girls made up dramatic episodes for the characters to act out and made the necessary costume changes as the drama unfolded. There were other "funnies" that were printed in little dots of color that worked like water colors when wet. Mum would make us brushes out of matchsticks with a bit of cotton batting twisted on the end, like the Q-tips people have today, and with an egg cup of water to dip the brushes into, we could spend a happy day carefully wetting and coloring these. Ethel invented another way to while away the winter evenings and weekends. She read to us as we gathered cosily in front of the kitchen oven, but at that time *The Canadian Reader* from school was about the only book available. Sometimes in the evening we listened to the radio, but that was before radio's golden age, so the programs were nothing much and the reception was unreliable and often spoiled by static, so we lost interest after the novelty wore off.

But when spring arrived it was as if I came to life just as everything else seemed to. Those trees along the road were filled with nesting birds chasing each other through the branches or sitting up high in the morning sun to sing challenges at their rivals for mates and living space. At least once a day I patrolled the trees monitoring progress. There were three nests of kingbirds gobbling up beaksful of grasshoppers and sawflies for their nestlings. Kingbirds are also called flycatchers, but kingbird is a better name because of their pretty, little reddish crowns. All along the barbwire fence against the road were more grasshoppers and toads and even mice that had been hung there on the steel barbs by two families of butcher birds (Northern Shrikes), birds that look like and play the part of their common name. High up in a slender branch of one of the limber kinds of trees I watched a pair of Baltimore Orioles weave their nest. The beautiful black-and-orange male flew back and forth carrying bits of string and grass and tufts of horsehair which he, on the outside, and the female, on the inside, wove and knotted together. When the last knot was tied and the last wisp tucked in, their nest hung like a weather-tight sack swaying even in the gentlest breeze. Beyond the tumbledown barn, three kinds of blackbirds wove grass nests among the bulrushes and wolf willows at the shore of a little slough. And there were plenty of slim crows shouting sharp alarms whenever I came near their bundle-of-stick nests way up in the highest trees.

For a while a big horned owl hung around and usually perched on a fence post near one end of the row of trees. We kids had been told that if you kept circling about an owl its eyes would follow you and its head would twist off. We tried it several times but we had to take our eyes off the bird in order to navigate some of the obstacles and so we were never quite sure that the owl's head stayed with us. But it sure did seem to, although its head never dropped off and it usually flew away after we'd made one or two trips around it.

The hired man from down the road came one day with four horses pulling a seed drill and I watched them plod steadily out to the back of the field and then back. At each return trip the man stopped to fill up the drill's seed box from a wagon that had appeared next to the fence and was half-filled with wheat smelling sweetly of formaldehyde. At each pass the seed drill's disks opened about twenty shallow furrows for the seeds that tumbled down flexible tubes, and twenty chains dragging behind pulled the earth back over them. I hung around nearby, pretending to be interested in snaring a gopher with a bit of binder twine, but keeping an eye on his interesting movements. Sometimes the man rode standing on the narrow wooden platform along the back of the seed drill, and then he would seem to tire of riding and jump down to stride along in the loose earth as the horses continued their slow march. I guess he found the job boring, but when he sort of let me climb up with him on the platform, I hunched my shoulders over the seed box to hold on and I thought it was wonderful.

The horses were Clydes, as most of the farm horses were. Clydes had a reputation for being gentle to manage and hard workers even on scanty feed. These were like that. They plodded on, up and down the field, with little urging. Their big, bay backsides rocked side to side as their big, hairy hoofs sank into the yielding earth to thrust the huge bodies steadily forward. A sharp horse smell rose and mingled with the earthy mushroom odor of the spring earth, attracting fierce, yellow "bulldogs" (horseflies) in spite of the four constantly swishing tails and the little skin shivers that horses use to ward them off. Once in a while, a big one would manage to penetrate the tough hide and, if undisturbed, could quickly fill up to bursting with rich horse blood. When he saw a fly within reach, the hired man would try to smack it with an end of one of the long, leather lines. He was quite expert at it, and the horses seemed to understand the difference between the smack to kill a horsefly and the smack that told Jess or Dolly or Barney or Prince to step up the pace a bit.

Later, as the weather warmed and life burgeoned, I became a bit more adventurous and began exploring the empty buildings in the yard. There were two or three granaries alive with mice and full of their pungent smell. On a shelf in the barn, I found a robin's nest made of mud and grass and with four beautiful blue eggs. Some animal had dug several entrance holes under one of the granaries. It was likely a skunk so I didn't go back around that one.

Even before winter lost its grip we put earth into the flat, wooden boxes which had come from Eaton's catalogue in the fall filled with smoked fish, and we planted pepper grass in them to grow for salad greens in the windows of one of the upstairs bedrooms. By the time for outdoor planting, I guess my dad had got word of his move to Laura because we didn't plant a garden. But we did dig up along the west side of the house and put in nasturtiums and scarlet runner beans. My parents used the nasturtium leaves like lettuce and we kids used to pick the flowers and suck the nectar out of the long, pointed reservoir on the bottom. The beans grew nearly up to the roof by the end of June, but then it was time to pack everything up again. My dad took one hayrack load to Laura, and the next day we loaded up the rest and we all left together, Dad with the hayrack, and my older brother driving Mum and us kids and a few odds and ends in the Model T. By the time Dad arrived about noon we had the cookstove set up and dinner ready so he could return the borrowed horses and hayrack to Donavon while Harold followed with the Model T to bring him back.

The first thing I remember doing at our new home was running barefoot around the house and stepping on a nail in a chunk of board hidden in the grass.

Music, music, music

I expect that, like Laura, most communities must have had quite a few members who knew how to play some instrument, even if only a mouth organ or a kazoo, and although they never really got together formally to make an orchestra, they were usually ready to sit down with whoever else was present and create a danceable rendition of "Five Foot Two, Eyes of Blue," or "Lulu's Back in Town." Still, an old-timer once told me of being at a house party where nobody showed up who had an instrument or knew how to play one. Not disheartened, the folks just took turns joining a leader who clapped out a rhythm and the dancing started at nine and was still going at four the next morning. There must have been some mighty sore hands milking the cows when they got home.

With what passed for music teaching in the schools it's a wonder kids learned to make any kind of music. It seems to me it was the older people who made our music and few of them passed it on. My mother had been a music teacher in England but she gave up on me after the second go. Still, both my sisters learned from her and in the church at Laura they sometimes played the little foot-pumped organ for the Sunday School hymns.

At Frontenac School Mr. Hartridge taught guitar music but I don't remember that he had a guitar. I never knew what all that business of squares with dots in them was all about at the time. I discovered, years later when I was a teen-ager, that it must have been guitar music. But, generally, schools came equipped with a dingus called a blackboard liner. This was a wooden stick with five wire holders spaced along it to hold sticks of chalk so you could draw five parallel lines at once. There was the odd school that boasted a piano and some even had a teacher who could play it, but usually with the aid of nothing more than a blackboard liner and the ability to draw recognizeable freehand treble clefs, our teachers drilled away at us until some of us, before we even reached high school, could recite "Every good boy does fine" and "f-a-c-e" and stick 'em on the lines in more or less the right places. Once we'd made it into high school we escaped from music and went into French in much the same manner and with almost equal success.

We always did do a lot of singing, most of it bloody awful, but we didn't know the difference. The persistence and the sheer heroics of the teachers and the CGIT leaders who whipped us into shape for the regular school and church-run concerts were amazing—talk about silk purses! Bassos were hard to find to really carry off "Grandfather's Clock" in style, but my sister Connie could sing a very noticeable alto in the CGIT girls' rendition of "Bells of Saint Mary's."

Teacher's announcement that we were going to have a session of singing always evoked a disorderly clamor with everyone shouting or rooting for a favorite ditty, and teacher trying to fob us off with "Sweet and Low" or "Swanee River" when the majority was clearly for "Oh! Susannah," or better still, "Polly Wolly Doodle All Day." We'd never heard of racism. We just practiced it. The only black man we saw was the porter we sometimes glimpsed when the six o'clock train stopped to chuck off the mail. So in spite of our general shortage of tonsils we rattled the roof shingles when we got to the verse that went:

> I came to a river and I couldn't get across.
> Singin' Polly Wolly Doodle all day.
> So I jumped on a nigger 'cause I thought he was a hoss.
> Singin' Polly Wolly Doodle all day.

And another favorite:

> I had a little nigger and he wouldn't grow no bigger
> So I put him in a music show.
> But he fell out of the winder and he broke his little finger
> And he couldn't play the old banjo.

Of course it was just ignorant. We were all pretty much that way— kids, teachers, parents, and all. We kids and our teachers were untravelled and deprived. Our parents came from lands where they'd grown up in the certain knowledge that their land was superior to all others, and that all of its well-deserved greatness had come about as the natural consequence of the innate wisdom, strength, intelligence, religious affiliation, or virtue of its inhabitants or of the quality of climate, vegetables, colonial possessions and rulers, or slaves it boasted.

But it was destructive, for it must have clung to us like a tick burrowing into a soft, neglected place and making poison, so that we never feel perfectly comfortable with people of other races no matter what kindness and what courtesy and good will they may have shown us or what allowances they have made for our shortcomings.

At Kinley, my dad had got us one of those big, floor-model wind-up gramophones, but all I can remember about it is that he traded it in for a peanut-tube radio with two sets of earphones. He took the earphones apart and made a couple more head-clamps so that we could have four single earphones instead of the two doubles. People sat up half the night listening to these things and keeping logs of the stations they brought in so that they could brag about them next day in the poolroom. There was KOA Denver, Colorado, and Davenport, Iowa. But the sets brought in so much static that the music was seldom good and there was not much else to listen for except the Winnipeg grain prices and the news.

Once in a while we would visit friends who had kept their gramophones, and we kids, or I, at least, would drive them batty playing through their entire record library four or five times without coming up for air. "Listen to the Mocking Bird" was a favorite, along with "Valencia," "The Whistler and His Dog," and "The Girl From Barcelona." And there were singers Billy Jones and Ernie Haire, and a guy named Wendell Hall who called himself "The Red-headed Music Maker." At one house they had a dozen or so Harry Lauder records, and although the parents were strict teetotallers, a favorite from that collection was "I Belong To Glasgow."

Besides being famous as the only town between Saskatoon and Kindersley that was built on both sides of the track, Laura also boasted a covered rink that was, I believe, the first outside the five cities in the province. Someone got hold of a record player that played single 78s electronically through a big speaker to skate by. Wow! Could you ever glide cross-handed with your girl when they played "It's Three O'clock in the Morning."

But the best music of all continued to be homemade, and as the Dirty Thirties rolled in, people made dances in the Orange Hall at five or ten cents admission—ladies bring lunch—to the music of the Ridge family band. Or sometimes it was Art Miller bouncing on the stool as he ripped out "Has Anybody Seen My Gal?" on the out-of-tune piano. Merle Trask was always willing to play his saxophone if the dancers could chip in thirty-five cents for a new reed, and if the reed arrived in the mail in time from Saskatoon. Gordon Moncrief called the squares and the old floor would bounce so that it threatened to give way at any minute, but nobody worried about it because they knew it was only a foot or so above the ground.

How devastating to see Laura now: the derelict hulk of the once-so-busy skating rink, with caved-in roof, hesitating a moment before it falls into a heap of rotting lumber amid the cattails by the slough that used to supply the water for its ice-maker; a remnant of the General Store's warehouse, still in its original metal cladding, making it recognizable amid a patch of tall weeds; hardware store gone; restaurant gone; poolroom and barbershop gone; blacksmith shop gone; Red and White Store and post office vaporized; garage, once the winter refuge of a dozen Smear-players, obliterated; two-roomed school empty, its belfry plundered of the bell that daily used to call sixty-odd kids to class until its rope fell in a loose pile on the floor one day and was never replaced; United Church pried loose from its foundation and dragged across the block to serve some new un-Christian enterprise long since abandoned; Orange Hall, where we danced, disappeared and the music silenced.

King of the castle

Today, I would likely be called "chicken." After we moved to Laura it was a couple of years before I ventured to cross the tracks and investigate "the other side of town." Steam trains frequently roared through the dividing line, carrying coal and gravel to God knows where, or rattled into town to shunt boxcars, battering empties into place and towing out the loaded cars along the side track next to the elevators. Sometimes the engines would stand panting at the station, dripping and steaming and making ominous breathing sounds deep in their innards, threatening any minute to relieve explosive pressures by loosing scalding jets of steam to engulf small boys. The freights' empty boxcars usually carried "bums" lurking in their dark interiors, and who could tell what they might do to a nosy kid who got too close?

On the farm at Donavon I'd never go upstairs to the empty rooms unless someone went with me, and when I went near the outbuildings looking for bird nests or whatever, my stomach hurt and I was tense and ready to run if a ferocious animal or a bat or burglar snuck up on me.

At Norquay School, where my fourteen-year-old brother Harold drove us in the T-model, I was frightened of two things. The worst was the likelihood of having to go to the toilet, which was one of those pail-type affairs smelling of some strong chemical, among other things. It was located in the porch of the school and the door used to stick so

I couldn't open it. If I failed to get it open, and asked to go a second time, the teacher wouldn't let me and I had to sit there terrified. Almost as terrifying was a game some of the big boys invented called "Walk the Plank." They had a long plank, probably ripped out of the school barn, and they wedged one end and propped up the middle over a piece of log. In the game they blindfolded the little kids and made them walk up the slope, trying not to overbalance and fall sideways. The kids then had to anticipate reaching the end of the plank so they could jump the two or three feet to the ground instead of taking an extra step into thin air and getting up out of the dust with a bloody nose or a lacerated knee. Fortunately for me, I got the whooping cough and missed a couple of weeks or so of that torment.

At Laura two different recurrent nightmares terrified me for a year or more until I would wake up from them in a pool of sweat, with my heart threatening to burst through my ribs and my lungs seeming paralyzed and deflated. The dreams only stopped when I began to realize, halfway to their climaxes, that they really were only dreams and that when I woke there would be no one standing over me waiting to fasten his hands around my throat, or that I hadn't really turned into a boatman beetle swimming in McCurdy's Slough.

But at other times I was a little bastard, and I usually got into some stupid activity because I was challenged and full of Dutch courage. At Donavon the storekeeper had a boy about my age, going on six, and a girl about three. We were playing in the yard behind the store one Saturday morning and he suggested we should lift his sister up so she could grab hold of the clothesline. Once we'd conned her into letting us do that, we ran away and left her there, screaming her head off.

Soon after we moved to Laura, I suddenly realized that I was big for my age and very strong and wiry. I began to take fiendish pleasure for a few years in bossing littler kids around and frequently, for no reason, wrestling them down and forcing them to say "I give up!" before I would let them go. I became a quick-tempered bully, too. Once, at a school picnic, with all the mothers watching, I cracked another kid over the head with a china school cup when he moved into my place after I'd got up to get more lunch. I don't understand now why I did that, and I guess I didn't understand it then, either. The kid was low down on the pecking order, but I didn't dislike him, and I didn't really much care where I sat.

But it might have been something to do with changes that were occurring and that I was only half aware of. For one thing, I had organized a gang—three or four younger kids that I hung out with and pushed around. Bloated with ego and a sense of power I got the conceited idea that I was so well loved that I should bring democracy to my subjects and take a vote to confirm my regal station. What a humiliatin' experience! They voted three to one for the skinniest, wimpiest kid in the group. It was my first confrontation with the treacherous nature of the downtrodden. I was so deflated that it took days before I let my temper loose and whipped them back into submission.

Then, almost overnight, another disaster. I looked around in the schoolyard and found that nearly all those runts and peewees had shot upward and grown muscles while my hormones seemed to have dried up and left me much the same size as I'd been last year. One day when I was in the middle of a tussle, trying to reassert my power, the two biggest ruffians in the school dragged me off and dumped me headfirst down a hole that had been dug for a new gate post. Luckily they were too scared of what the teacher might do if they left me there as I deserved, so they dragged me out when the bell rang.

I reacted to my overthrow much as a rooster faced with recognizing a new cock of the barnyard. I found a place somewhere in the middle of the dominance order from which I could still pick on a few of the outcasts, but generally I fell in with the hellery proposed by the leaders. Like the time a gang of us were walking along the tracks when one kid threw a rock that smashed a telegraph line insulator, then somebody else heaved a boulder straight up so that it came down with a delicious crunch, like a sledge hammer dropped on an ice-cube, and we ended up smashing so many insulators that all the wires were hanging loose for a quarter mile. How or why the section foreman covered up for us remains a mystery to me, but he must have been a kindlier man than any of us kids ever pictured him. We should have landed in jail.

Demolition days

My mum generally despaired of me. She usually called me "The Human Garbage Pail" because I ate everything in sight. At the table I cleaned up everything that was left over, and between times, I ate my fingernails and the corners torn from books and newspapers I was reading. In the spring I would go out and pick two big water pails of tender pigweed tops and after my mum cooked them I'd hardly let anyone else have more than a taste.

My favorite, though, was beans. Put me down to a table set with a big pot of home-baked beans with a ham hock in the middle and you'd be lucky to get a spoonful. One evening nobody else had an appetite for the beans steaming deliciously before us so I was able to clean up three servings and then scrape out the pot. It was heaven.

At least it was until about midnight when I woke up with a bellyache. By dawn I felt sure I was going to explode. My tummy was so distended that a pinprick would have sent me on a crazy rocket trip into space. Mum, who usually had to see a black-robed angel hovering before she thought we might be sick enough to stay home from school, gave in the minute she saw me. But then again, maybe she was thinking what would happen if I blew out all the windows of the classroom or stripped the shingles off the roof.

Anyway, as the morning passed so did my affliction, and Mum chanced sending me back to school and out into the rest of what Laura offered in the way of polite society. The next time we had beans I cut myself down to two platesful.

Another reputation I earned with Mum was of being a wrecker. But that was, as they used to say in the "Doc Savage" or "The Shadow" stories, "a bum rap." Sure I busted nearly everything I laid hands on, but that was because I was either fixing it, making it work better, or just trying to do a good deed. After my overthrow as dictator, I had moved suddenly in the opposite direction and developed a compelling sense of wanting to please everybody and of hating injustice, pain, and anything that seemed to me unfair.

In the beginning I had got into trouble through a compulsive fascination with texture, malleability, feel, taste, shape, and such qualities of things I encountered. Not everyone else seemed to understand this.

Except, maybe my dad.

I remember when I was just six, at the farm near Donavon, I found a big steel bolt with a square head around the outbuildings and was carrying it up to the house in case it might be useful for something. Before I got there I passed my dad's Model T and, for no reason, I scraped the bolt-head down the radiator, which was right out there on the front of the car, not hidden behind a fancy grill the way they are now. Radiators are made of copper tubes threaded through thin ribbons of copper metal cooling fins, and copper bends very easily.

Scraping the bolt down the radiator bent those copper ribbons, and I became conscious for the first time of the unspeakable excitement generated by discovering a scientific property of matter that I had up to now been oblivious to—the pliability of metals.

Unlike Newton or Watt, I didn't immediately move from the theoretical to the practical to invent the wire coat hanger, or else my dad's rad might not have boiled over next day on his way to town. He must have found time at the elevator to straighten the fins back out because they got straightened, and the only thing that happened was he looked severely at me and wondered out loud how they got bent.

Years later, as I grew up to become one of the peons, I slowly came to realize another of life's truths: that some of us attract blame while others shed it like water from a muskrat's fur. It's a bit like in the English music-hall song:

Hit's thuh syme thee 'ole world owver,
Hit's thuh poor wot gets thee blyme,

Woile thee rich gets all thee pleasure,
Now, ayen't that a bleedin' shyme?

The Laura School (Helena School District) was well built. It remains standing after sixty-odd years while the rest of the town, except a couple of elevators, has disappeared or fallen into ruin among the pigweeds and Russian thistles. Its doorways were all trimmed with six-inch-wide boards of the best fir, stained, and varnished. But school doorways, no matter how vigilant the teachers or their tattletale informants, take a lot of abuse, and fir lumber can get really splintery and dangerous after a few years of contact with stepladders, ball bats, chemical toilet buckets, and snow shovels.

I noticed one doorway with an ugly split starting and threatening to develop into a sharp spear that I imagined impaling some rowdy student jostling through the mob at recess. I had acquired a jackknife by this time and so I began to do my civic duty by cutting away the loose splinter and rounding off the stump. But just then a teacher came along and talk about being misunderstood!

But nobody ever threatened to call in parents or make them pay for the damage when the farm boys, who all owned expensive, stag-handled, brass-bound jackknives with castrating blades and everything, put four holes clean through the fir flooring and halfway through the next layer in the front entryway playing a game they called "knife," but which, I think, is properly known as "mumblety-peg."

And neither was teacher curious about all the girls' screams and giggles the day a boy came to school with a pig's tail in his pocket and stood in the door of the girls' cloakroom with it hanging out the fly of his bib overalls. Or where was teacher the time she kept a bunch of us boys in at recess and one boy went round and peed in all the inkwells while the rest of us laughed our heads off?

Another time I was mooching about in the elevator at noon. There was a maintenance gang there doing repairs and they were off somewhere eating their dinner. My dad must have still been home, too. Anyway, everybody knows what a pain sparrows are around an elevator. My dad used to take his pellet gun and clean them out every so often. Well, I happened to be climbing up the ladder that's nailed to the leg, a wooden enclosure where the conveyor belt with the grain cups on it runs from bottom to top. The cups pick up grain from the pit under the scales and lift it to the cupola at the top where it is dumped into the particular bin it's to be stored in. It's about sixty feet to the top, but I was only about halfway up when I saw this sparrow nest just out of reach on a ledge.

With one foot as far over on the rung as I could slide it, and hanging on by one hand, I could almost reach the nest, but however I stretched and maneuvered I just couldn't get hold of it to pull it down. Then I saw this piece of two-by-four sticking out nearby. It was toenailed into a cleat on the bin wall, and braced underneath with a three-foot chunk of inch-thick shiplap. It seemed to me to be just the thing!

I carefully moved over onto it, holding myself to the bin wall with my palms flattened against it, and, by golly! I snatched that nest loose and let it fall. Then I eased myself back onto the ladder and looked down to see the nest just hitting the floor below.

But, oh, oh! Four Scandinavian carpenters suddenly appeared looking up at me, and they didn't look as if they were waiting to present me with the Nobel Prize.

They weren't.

It took me sixty years to realize why I insulted the boss. A superintendent, known to us kids as "the boss," used to come around about once or twice a year on a sort of inspection trip of the elevator to make sure the agent was not goofing off or short-weighing anybody, especially the company. When the boss came, the agent usually invited him home for dinner. After all, what else could he do?

Anyway, this particular year, the boss happened to come on December eighth, my eighth birthday, and after we'd eaten (he wouldn't have any of my mum's delicious bread pudding, so I got to finish it up), he and Dad went into the front room to relax before going back to work.

It was customary at our house for us kids to be given our birthday presents right after dinner before going back to school, so the small stir aroused by the presentation in the kitchen drew the boss's attention and he called me in before him. I was quite nervous because I thought maybe he was mad at me for making so much noise, and I stood wondering what was next when he pulled a half-dollar out of his pocket and pressed it into my hand and wished me a happy birthday.

Did I say, "Thank you very much, sir"? Did I become inarticulate and run? Not me! Not the poor sap who always did something stupid.

I said, "Aw, it's not much!"

Back in the kitchen, my mum was horrified. The other kids gave me looks that said, "There he is. He's done it again!" And Mum made me go back in to the front room and say my thanks.

But the reason I never understood saying that was because fifty cents was really quite a lot of money. It was so much that I don't think the boss could have even got away with putting it down on his expense account as payment for a meal. You could get a full course meal complete with finger bowls at the Elite Cafe in Saskatoon for thirty-five cents.

I was stunned. I'm sure I had never held such an enormous amount of money in my hand in all my life. And there were my sisters and my little brother, who never had the luck to get a birthday when the boss was around, all peeking through the half-open door and thinking, Why him? Why him?

So what could I do? I had to say something to make them feel better, and felt I had to say it right away.

If only I'd said, "Thank you very much, sir," to the boss, and then turned and fled back to the kitchen and shut the door behind me before I said, "Aw, it's not much!" Mum and the others might have understood. They might have been jealous, who could blame them? But I think they'd have understood, and I'd have come off as a great brother instead of a boob.

So, as I've said, I only just realized why I did it, and my mum and dad and all the rest of them except Connie have gone to their graves never finding out at all.

How pleasant
it is to have money!

Money was scarce. Up until I was twelve I got an allowance of a nickel a week. I didn't have to do anything for it, but at Laura I did try to help out because the other kids around town had chores to do and I didn't want to be odd man. I cleaned out the chicken house, gathered eggs, split up the scrap lumber my dad usually got left from repair work on the elevator or the company house, brought in kindling, carried two buckets of water hanging on the handlebars of my bike from McCurdy's artesian well, and straightened used nails for my dad to build another four feet onto the garage when we got the '29 Plymouth. One family gave their kids a dime a week but then some didn't get anything.

But once in a while the chance came along to earn something, occasionally through wit, but more likely by sweat. It was by wit that I earned my first pay.

I was four and a half or so, and I went into Joe Tate's store in Kinley because I wanted to ask him for an apple box. I was going to use the wheels off my older brother Harold's tricycle to make a wagon, and I figured an apple box would be just the thing to complete the job. Joe was a bachelor, and I suppose he must have got a bit lonely at times, so he liked kidding around with people. He looked down at me from behind his long, country-store counter and challenged me that I didn't know how to make a wagon. I said that I sure did, and it ended up that he accused me of not even knowing the directions. Well, I did know them, and I pointed them out to him and a couple of amused onlookers – north, south, east, and west.

Joe was so fascinated that he not only went out back and found me a nice, clean box, still smelling sweetly of Macintosh apples, but he took the lid off a candy jar and dug out for me the biggest piece of ribbon candy I'd ever seen.

My next experience with earning a living was more in the sweat category with a measure of anxiety and terror thrown in, making it prophetic of real life as I've known it. It was a few months later, and I and a couple of bigger kids had been messing about around the Kinley elevators. We stumbled onto about two bushels of wheat that had got spilled beneath the spout that hangs out the trackside wall of the elevator for loading boxcars. At first we stomped around in it a bit, but then somebody got the idea to gather it up and sell it to Mr. Squires, the hotel keeper, for his chickens.

We found a gunnysack somewhere, and one of the others went for his wagon (mine had not been all that successful), and we scraped up the wheat and delivered it to the hotel. Mr. Squires was so pleased that he gave us a dime apiece. It was the first dime I ever owned and I pressed it tight into my hand and made a fist around it so I could take it home to show my mum.

But the other kids were a bit more blasé, and they were tossing their dimes from hand to hand and trying to out-brag each other about the selection of candy they were going to get at the Chinese cafe. Of course the inevitable happened. One of the dimes popped out of a hand, hit a plank in the board sidewalk, rolled tantalizingly along it a second, and then dropped through the crack, out of sight and irretrievable.

I saw their eyes meet, a quick nod of agreement, and I took off with the two of them full tilt at my heels aiming to replace the lost dime at my expense. I must have run like a jackrabbit because I kept ahead of them the couple of blocks or so to the kitchen screen door that I slammed in their faces just in time.

When I was twelve I got a steady job. Mrs. McCurdy, who ran the Red and White Store and post office at Laura, hired me at a dollar a week to carry the mail six nights a week from the six-twenty train. I used a neat little wheelbarrow for that because the incoming load was often heavy with parcels from Eaton's and Simpson's. At Christmas time it was sure to be, sometimes enough for three or four loads. Once a month or so I earned an extra fifteen cents if I could beat the drayman and haul over the Red and White Store's order of groceries that came in on the express car of the same train. But I never saw any of that except to carry it home, because I handed it over to Mum, and from then on I bought my clothes from it and saved enough to have a small stake for the day when I left home six years later.

I was lucky. Jobs for wages were mostly non-existent. Once when I was six or seven I spent the day snaring gophers with a farmer who was seeding, and when I left he handed me three or four letters and a handful of coins and asked me to mail the letters for him when I went past the post office on my way home. I checked the money and it was two nickles and five pennies and I figured I had such a bonanza I would be able to buy a Cherry Flip which I'd always coveted but would never buy because it seemed an extravagance if all you had was a nickle. But now I'd be able to get a Cherry Flip and still have ten cents left over to give my mum to save.

But there was no Cherry Flip at the end of my rainbow that day because Mrs. McCurdy pointed out that there were no stamps on the envelopes. She was unconvinced when I suggested that the farmer would probably be in in a few days to pay for them, and she finally wormed it out of me that he'd given me fifteen cents, of which twelve would buy four stamps, and I was actually two cents short of the going rate on Cherry Flips.

Another farmer got me to lead his horse all one afternoon while he came behind with a walking plow planting spuds. He didn't pay, but I think he did say, "Thanks." And a third one hired me and three other kids for two-bits each to dig and top carrots all day. He had planted two acres of carrots hoping to store them in pits until frost and then sell them in early winter to keep the wolf from the door. In the end, though, he pulled up stakes and moved in with a relative at "the coast," the carrots froze and were dug up and eaten by the plague of jackrabbits that appeared that year, and none of us kids ever did see our quarters.

I earned an honest quarter, though, and collected, by digging twenty-odd sacks of potatoes with another kid for the Laura garage proprietor and milkman. But by now I was a teen-ager, too smart ass to push the coin into my hand and make a fist around it. I stuck it in my shirt pocket, and I didn't even run straight home. Instead I went to investigate something that took me through a pagewire fence and back again and when I did finally get home I found my pocket empty.

Twenty bags of spuds and nothing to show for it! No way! I went back over in my mind where I'd gone to try and figure out where the quarter had slipped out of my pocket. I decided it had to have been where I'd crawled through the pagewire fence. It was getting near dusk but I went back and searched on my hands and knees in the grass until it was too dark to see any more.

Next day in school I was obsessed. It was bad enough to lose the money, but it was as bad to have been so stupid. Was I destined to be a klutz all my life? As soon as school was out I went back and searched again. I knew it had to be there, but darkness again came down on my search and I had to give up without success.

The following day there was an early snow. There was no use looking in that. The snow hung on, and winter set in in earnest. All winter I brooded periodically about that quarter that I was certain lay under the snow where it had dropped by the pagewire fence. But as the sun finally warmed and the snow shrank back to let the new green grass shoot through last year's matted brown, I guess my passion abated or was overwhelmed by the excitement of another prairie spring because I didn't resume my search.

But that spring faded early and there was no rain. In the school yard the base paths of the ball diamond wore to ruts an inch deep in dust. One day at recess a small cloud floated over and spattered just enough drops on the ball field to bring up that unforgettable smell of damp prairie earth. We stopped our game to breathe it into our parched lungs, and that was it. June came with a cruel sun to bake the earth and scorch the crops, and overnight a billion army worms appeared and cleaned off the surviving Russian thistle. They swarmed over the CNR rails in the morning and then flowed along the gravel ballast like a green river, trapped when the sun raised steel to the boiling point. Then in the evening, when the rails cooled, and they resumed their migration, their squirming bodies greased the track so that the mail train had to back up and take a second run up the rise to the west. The worms vanished overnight, and in their place a million billion grasshoppers appeared, also out of nowhere, and with the crops and the Russian thistle gone, they fell to devouring people's laundry hanging on the wash lines and leather harness and each other. Instead of spring breezes an ominous calm settled over the devastated land and then gradually turned to wind, and wind turned into dust storms. No drop of rain fell, and at noon the sun disappeared in the red sky, and the abrasive air burned throats and caked eyesockets with mud.

Sane men became despondent, and despondent men suicidal. My rage with my lost quarter returned and gnawed at me. Finally, one day, the storms stopped. The air became still again and the red, Texas dust settled along the fence wires and piled up atop the posts. That bloody quarter! It had to be there somewhere under the dead and dust-filled grass.

I went back to the fence and I crawled, raking through a square foot at a time until my bitten fingertips were sore and bleeding.

An hour or more passed. I was prepared to go on for another hour, another day—forever, by God! I was going to find that lousy quarter if it took the rest of my life.

But it didn't. Suddenly, unbelievably, there it was, black as soot but otherwise round and quarterish as a silver quarter could be. I hurried home and put it away in my dresser drawer. I intended to keep it, but a few weeks later all the emotion dissipated and I blew it at the last fair I think Laura ever had.

Plenty to do,
and drama, too

When Saskatchewan Wheat Pool started in 1925, it had only five elevators, my dad said, and the elevator he ran at Donavon was one of them. It must have been owned by one of the line companies before that and couldn't have been in very good shape because they built a new one soon after that. Then again it might have burnt down. Those wooden elevators were real susceptible to fires. Anyway, it happened after we left and moved to Laura, and I remember that we drove over there one Sunday to see the new one under construction.

The elevator at Laura was an old one, too, and it had a decided tilt to it. My dad had a chunk of iron tied to a rope that he let out the window of the cupola so that it hung down the side from the eave to measure the tilt. It started to get worse and people began to think it could go over and fall smash down on the coal sheds beside it. The Quaker Oats elevator had tipped over some years before, but it went right bang across the tracks and blocked them off for two or three days. People didn't think much of having another mess like that to clean up, even if it did miss the tracks and provide a few weeks' work for the town's loafers.

Anyway, after a year or two, the company sent a crew around in the summer to straighten the elevator up. They lifted it with big screw jacks, and then blocked it there with square timbers while they dug out the old foundation and made a new one.

At the same time, they put in a new steel pit and new scales and driveway. The operation provided the whole town with a couple of months' entertainment, and it was especially absorbing to us kids, who spent most of our daylight hours fascinated by it all.

One of the many town dogs was a little white fox terrier that spent its time out on the streets yipping and snapping at everyone's heels. In the winter time it used to run over the frozen ground alternating between its front feet and its back ones trying to keep them from freezing. It could run fifty feet or so on its two front legs with its back end hoisted up in the air, and then change ends and run like a little, white-furred man on its hind legs. Except for that, it had no other talent, and everybody hated it and wished curses on it.

One Friday, the repair gang finally got the new steel pit installed into its hole in the covered driveway, and on Saturday morning we kids all went to see if the job met our expectations. That little dog had yipped and yapped from one to another of us all the way, and had worked up a pretty fierce and fearless temper by the time we arrived. We moved up as close as we dared to the yawning steel-lined chasm, and darned if there wasn't a big weasel in there that must have been hunting mice during the night and fallen in. In the daylight anybody could see there was no way out of that pit once you were in it unless somebody let down a rope or something, but not that fool dog. It just leaped in at one of the sloping ends, landing about halfway down. And then, skidding the rest of the way on its stubbly tail, it somersaulted once and came up running. The weasel retreated to a corner momentarily, and then leaped out and buried its needle-sharp teeth in the dog's nose to the admiring cheers of the watchers. There it hung until somebody remembered where they could borrow a long ladder and climbed down into the pit to separate them. The dog was glad enough to be picked up and dumped out over the top, but the weasel, of course, had to be shot.

The reason for all the elevator problems was the unstable soil that the buildings stood on. It was gumbo clay. Although it seemed flat enough, the town was actually in a shallow depression with the water table pretty close to the surface and the stratum of gumbo holding it from rising up to flood us out.

If you dug a hole through the clay, you got an artesian well, which was nice if you could control the water. If you weren't careful digging holes, you could end up with a mosquito-infested swamp. There was a good artesian well right in the center of our side of town and it provided everybody around with good, cold water that ran down a ditch to McCurdy's Slough. A lot of people had a wooden box sunk into the ditch, with open ends to let the cold water run through and cool their milk and meat and such stuff.

The slough itself provided hours of fun for us kids, and ideal habitat for almost every kind of aquatic bird and animal life. In summer we spent hours wading through the bulrushes to find the nests of a dozen or more kinds of waterfowl. There were blue terns and curlews, three kinds of blackbirds, and a half-dozen kinds of ducks. Muskrats, tadpoles, toads and frogs, garter snakes, and a hundred varieties of bugs swam on, and under, the cool surface. And in the winter it was a free, full-time skating rink.

If anyone stuck a fence post into that ground, it started to work its way out again right away, and in a couple of years, you'd have to dig a new hole and sink it down again. Some people tried holding them down with rocks, but there weren't enough rocks around there to do much good.

Farm dogs were usually pleasant, gregarious beasts whose only duties were to guard the property from suspicious-looking characters and rustle up the cows if they were late coming in from the pasture. It was an easy life. There weren't really any suspicious-looking characters around, and the cows usually knew enough to come in when their udders were full. So most of the time farm dogs had only to wag their tails if somebody gave them a pat, and to come when they were called, if they happened to feel like it. But on Saturdays, farm dogs sometimes got confused.

Farmers usually came to town in some kind of horse-drawn vehicle on Saturdays, and the farm dogs liked to come along, trotting away in the shade between the back wheels. By mid-afternoon there'd be buggies and democrats, and the odd wagon and saddle horse tied up to every telephone pole along the street. Under most of them you'd find a farm dog snoozing with his tail curled up in front of him, and opening one eye now and then to check out the situation. Most of the time the dogs stayed put, pretending to guard the vehicle, but once in a while, one would get tired of that and decide to get up and go home, or take a turn around the town to see what was doing. That's usually when all hell would break loose. Some other guard dog, or one of the town dogs, would spot him and charge, and then just about every dog in the place would come tearing up to get into the fight. We kids would always come running, too, to watch. If we were lucky, the dogfight would send one of the horses crazy. He'd break loose from where he was tied along the board sidewalk and turn for home taking the back wheels off the buggy next to him as he went by. That could start a chain reaction that would have maniac horses galloping out of all three exits from town, with the remnants of smashed vehicles, egg crates, cream cans, butter boxes, and harness littering the trail for a mile or more behind them. A melee like that would provide occasion for eye-witness, tall, bragging, and one-upmanship stories to last us kids and the town loafers clear into the next season.

Late fall was always welcome, even if it did mean we'd soon have to get out the long johns. It was because of the fowl suppers. Once people got cars they could attend four or five fowl suppers around the nearby towns and the country schools. It was the main way to raise money for the Christmas concert or the church, but it wasn't really very practical. In the first place, all the women had to roast chickens and ducks and turkeys and bake pies and layer cakes and bread; they boiled and mashed potatoes, set jellied salads, and brought up jars of pickles and saskatoons from the cellars; and when they had enough to fill up the washboiler and two or three washtubs and a cardboard box, they hauled it to the town hall, or the church, or the schoolhouse, and donated it in. Then, from five o'clock until midnight or later, they stayed on to serve and reheat and slice and butter and refill, because it they didn't, there'd be sure to be somebody disparaging their contribution behind their backs.

The kids and the men would all come and eat like pigs – three plates of meat and potatoes with big helpings of peas and pickles and salad, one piece each of apple and saskatoon and pumpkin pie, a goodly dollop of cream on each, and one slice of chocolate layer cake and a two-inch square of six or seven other kinds to finish off with, and five or six cups of coffee just to wash it all down. If there was anything left that was still edible, the ladies could sit down for twenty minutes about ten o'clock to finish it off, but, of course, they were expected to pay in their thirty-five cents just like the men. We kids usually paid a quarter.

So, if they served two hundred people, the sponsors would net a clear sixty bucks, and not a penny went out for expenses.

Just to make sure that the fowl suppers wouldn't be the last chance to enjoy a gastronomic blowout until spring, most people got in a good supply of meat every fall. A lot of people raised some, especially chickens, in their back yards, but you could arrange with a farmer friend to bring you beef, pork, or lamb, or ducks, geese, and turkeys when he did his butchering. People that liked fish could order frozen fresh-water fish that came from Big River, up north, through ads in *The Western Producer*. And from Eaton's catalogue you ordered your smoked or salted cod and herrings that were caught in the Atlantic.

My dad usually bought a side of beef, a whole pig, a lamb, and one or two turkeys—and a goose, if he could find one. He'd order a hundred pounds of whitefish and fifty of jacks, and a twenty-five-pound box each of smoked cod and kippers. We usually had a dozen or so roosters from our own flock as well. All this was cut and wrapped on the kitchen table by the light of a kerosene lamp, and then we'd put it out in the porch to freeze before tossing it all into our galvanized rain barrel and a big gasoline drum, out on the north porch. There was a wooden lid on each barrel, with a two-foot chunk of railroad iron holding it down in case a stray dog came by.

After the fowl suppers and getting in the meat, there was no really big excitement until the Christmas concert. That was pretty exciting for the little kids and for the parents, but it was an anxious, tearful exercise for the school kids, who'd spent weeks rehearsing play parts, marching drills, and comic recitations, and hadn't got them to please the teacher once. In Kinley there were two churches and they each ran their own shows. They took up a collection from the parishioners, and all I can remember about it was the bag of candy you got from Santa Claus. It was much the same at Donavon, except that they held the party in the afternoon at our church, and they had Santa Claus waiting in one of the elevators until the train came in so he could board it out of sight and come waltzing off onto the station platform, as if he'd just come out from Saskatoon. At the church hall they had a tree with candles on it, and Santa got his cotton batting beard too close and had to dash out the door in mid ho-ho-ho to extinguish the fire in a snowbank.

At Laura there was only one church, so the concert was a blockbuster extravaganza with all the combined musical and dramatic talent of three schoolrooms, the CGIT, the church choir, and two or three volunteer pianists put on display. It was too big to be accommodated by any of the schoolrooms or the church. Nothing but the Orange Hall could begin to accommodate it, and even then, some latecomers had to watch through the side windows or the open back door.

But the first Laura concert was a big disappointment to me. Instead of taking up a collection to provide something for each kid, the parents each brought presents for their own. The highlight of the whole thing, when Santa appeared to pass out the gifts, was an insensitive and ostentatious display of affluence, with a few kids surrounded by a wall of packages while three or four of Santa's helpers tore back and forth delivering more. The rest of us strained to hear our own names called out above the racket, and when the tension culminated in a quick exit by the perspiring Saint Nicholas impersonator, most were left clutching one or two little gewgaws, wrapped in red or green tissue paper. A few, including the Macklon kids, whose parents hadn't been approached, sat empty-handed, and in my case, at least, mad as hell.

Come to the fair

I don't remember any fairs until we moved to Laura, but from then on, fairs were highlights of the year—even better than Christmas. There used to be a lady in Saskatoon that we heard on the radio now and then, and I saw her on the stage once between the double features at the movies. They were putting on some kind of a civic performance to show how cosmopolitan and cultured the city was becoming, having a population of thirty-five thousand and Ben Hoeschen's brewery and Quaker Oats and all. She was known, I think, as Madame Sherry or Cherry—something like that—and she was probably a pretty good singer. However most of us people at Laura didn't have the sophistication to appreciate the classical stuff she sang except I think we all stayed tuned whenever she sang "Come to the Fair," which she seemed to do often. "Da, da, da to welcome the day," she would sing, "and it's heigh-ho, come to the fair!" Wow! We didn't need any urging.

The new rink, which had just come through its first winter season, became the venue for presentation of the Sixtieth Anniversary of Confederation medals to all the school kids in 1927. Some time in June, I think, the teachers herded us all down there, where we found a platform set up all decorated with flags and bunting, and a group of dignitaries, including the local MP, Mr. Loucks, all the way from Delisle, eager to inflict a half-hour of patriotic speeches on us in the vain expectation that their words would be inscribed, if not in the history books, then at least in the memories of those present. As soon as they let us out, most of us drilled or punched holes through the medals with some vague notion that we would hang them on something.

As soon as they got that cleared away a crew set to work building trestles and stands and tables and racks. Somewhere they found a hundred wire poultry cages and set them up, and sawdust and straw were spread in the muddy spots where the ice had been. And that was just the indoor exhibits. Small animal pens built of poles and slabs and shaded by leafy poplar branches appeared out back of the rink on the fairgrounds, and proprietors built four or five refreshment booths. Somebody loaned their four-horse team to pull the municipal grader around the racetrack. The chicken-wire backstop of the ball diamond was repaired and extended, and all the gopher holes were filled in. It was fair time!

Next day, soon after daylight, the exhibitors began arriving. First came horse-drawn wagons bringing fat porkers and sheep or sleek beef and dairy cattle to be herded down the cleated loading chute and into the waiting pens. Buggies and democrats crowded in, leading prize Clydesdales, Percherons, and Belgians with their manes braided and tied with little red bows for the show. By ten every space was parked solid with Fords and Chevvies, Dodges, Whippets – even a couple of Oldsmobiles and one Marmon.

Inside the rink farm wives filled the tables and racks with lace and embroidery and dresses and aprons, or with pies and cookies and cakes and loaves and plates of buns. There were jars full of pickles and jellied chicken and peach preserves and of saskatoons and vegetables – even bottles of chokecherry wine. Families proudly set up their green sheaves and glass sealers of wheat, oats, and barley, and of dry peas and beans and sunflower seeds.

Baseball started at ten on the diamond inside the racetrack, while around the perimeter tired and sweaty children wandered among the booths licking soggy ice cream cones and wiping the drips from their elbows on their skirts or overalls. If anybody had remained in the far reaches of town they could easily have heard the cheering and the crack of the old Louisville Sluggers driving grass-stained baseballs beyond the racetrack for homers. The sounds even rose above the music of a brass band brought in from somewhere especially for the occasion.

Soon after noon, some highbinder from the city appeared and set up a tent beside the entrance and started chucking out combs and pencils onto the grass around him. Then he started hollering through a megaphone to draw a crowd. It was impossible for a kid to get near enough to see what he was up to, but by about three o'clock some people had discovered that whatever he was selling either disintegrated or raised blisters or wouldn't cut butter or smelled worse than a dead skunk, so a few of the men packed him up and sent him on his way.

And right after that excitement died down we all went to the rink to shuffle up and down the rows of tables and cages and see who had won the ribbons and to marvel at the incompetence of the judges. Then it was back to the booths for a last Coca Cola or a cone of melting ice cream before searching out a spot in the stands to squeeze into, or a seat on the grass along the baselines, to watch the last two teams battle it out for the twenty dollar purse.

Out of sight inside the rink, exhausted women packed up their jars and bottles, and their needlework, and the sad-looking remnants of their once beautiful cookery. They pinioned their poultry and tied their legs, or pushed them into gunnysacks, for the journey home. Then when the kids and husbands fetched the buggies or the automobiles everybody pitched in to load it all up and sank, proud and contented, into the comfort of the horsehair-padded seats. Giddy up, Napoleon, it looks like rain.

The Laura and District Agricultural Society put on some fairs after that one, but they were never the same. People lost interest for some reason. Gradually it petered out until they quit using the rink—said they couldn't get it dried out in time. The animal pens fell to pieces and were carried away when some of the young blades laid out a six-hole golf course instead, and the plank stands behind the backstop disappeared.

For a few years the ball diamond continued in use. Tessier or Delisle or Donavon would come over for an evening game, but it was hard to take the league seriously. Sometimes the dozen or so fans, clutching their nickles or dimes brought for the collection, went home disappointed when the visitors failed to show.

Sky rockets,
girlie shows, and hard lessons

By the thirties people were more mobile because of so many cars. They were getting more sophisticated and choosy, too, or maybe they just figured it was too much work making a local fair that wasn't really all that glamorous any more. It was sure a lot less trouble to jump in the car and head off for Saskatoon, even if it was also a lot more expensive. At our house on the west edge of town, we kids could look out the upstairs window and see the fireworks going up thirty-odd miles away, but it was nothing like being right there in the grandstand. There, after the last fabulous act of the show had left the stage, the lights would go out, and suddenly in the outfield behind the stage a fiery Mountie would appear on a fiery horse, or a sparkling Union Jack would flutter between glowing images of the King and Queen. Then giant wheels of fire would start spinning crazily and hurling streams of dangerous-looking colored sparks, and lighting up the field where shadowy forms dashed about getting the sky rockets set.

Then it was magnificent! It was breathtaking—heart stopping! The rockets began to shoot up in twos and threes and explode against the blackness in showers of red, blue, green, and white fire. As the sparkles cascaded earthward they met the red hot trajectories of bigger, more fantastic rocketry, each burst outdoing the last until the show culminated in a pandemonium of explosion and flame and glitter that left us yokels spellbound and gasping. But the pyrotechnician hadn't finished with us yet. Allowing time only for a few deep breaths, he fired off a dozen of the kind that innocently spray a few streaks of color into the air and then detonate like a cannon—bang, bang, bang! Then, after a longer pause, an ear-splitting Big Bertha BOOM would shake the earth, threatening to bring down the grandstand in a heap of splinters. That was the signal for the crowd to rise from their seats and begin moving down, flowing like oil through a funnel, into the narrow ground-level space in front, where they shuffled and waited, shuffled and waited, shuffled and nearly took root, until at last they reached the gate and spread out into the midway. If you were a child, or even a small adult, you expected any minute to suffocate and fall under the feet of the mob.

In 1928 Harold left home to work for the Royal Bank at Dinsmore, so there were now just the four of us kids: Walter and me, hanging like death onto Dad's hands, and Connie and Ethel clinging to Mum. Whichever trio got through the gate first waited nearby for the others. Then, relieved to be safely together, and revived by the sudden freshness of the cool night air, we joined the crowd drifting along the midway. There, brilliant lights and spectacular colors had transformed the spinning wheels, the spiraling rides, and the beckoning sideshow fronts. The voices of barkers had acquired a new animation, their spiels more excitement and urgency. At the girlie shows the costumes seemed fresher and more vivid, and the girls plumper and prettier. All the noise and bustle urged us to linger, but we knew it was over, we had far to go. We'd slip through a gap into the semidarkness of the parking lot and wander along the rows until we stumbled on the car. Then Mum would pack us kids into the back seat to fall fast asleep, unaware of the bumps and mud holes along the forty-odd miles of dirt roads. In our dreams we were still at the fair, and in my own case, I was going in to see the half-man, half-woman, walking tip-toe tall because the barker had said, "No one under sixteen admitted."

The grandstand shows were amazing. Vaudeville was gone, at least the Canadian parts of the old circuits, so very few people had seen a stage show or any other kind of live performance except for the local Christmas concerts or school speech-making. We had a Chautauqua in Laura a time or two, but that was tame stuff. At the grandstand we saw clowns and tumblers, acrobats and daredevils, novelty musicians, boomerang throwers, high-wire acts, roller skaters, magicians, and sword swallowers. Every kid went back to his prairie village determined to get right to work learning to emulate some act in the show.

At Laura one of the older boys, Jack Darnborough, rigged up a trapeze in one of the barns. He even got hold of a pair of chaps and a gun belt and six-shooter that he swanked around town with for a week until somebody reported him to the town cop. Then he acquired a big hunting knife which he practiced throwing at fence posts and targets he'd chalked on the barn wall. The Darnboroughs were from England and were keen on amateur theatre and garden parties held in the grounds of their beautiful farmyard. During one of these parties, Jack took some of the men out to the barn to show off his accomplishments on the trapeze. He was hanging by his toes from the track used to hoist sling-loads of hay into the loft, when one of the watchers bet him he couldn't hang there for five minutes. It was early summer, so the loft was empty, leaving nothing under him but bare floor, but Jack took him on. Unfortunately he lost. Still, he must have learned some skills on the trapeze because he managed not to land on his head and he got up without any apparent fractures or dislocations.

The grandstand show inspired us all to great things. But the midway, apart from the rides, was pretty much an annual foray into the boondocks by Yankee con men out to fleece the greedy and the gullible. I heard lots of tales of farmers losing their shirts at the crown and anchor wheel, but never one of a farmer going home with enough winnings to lift the mortgage. On the other hand, many of us kids learned a few things about life that we couldn't have discovered out behind the barn. For example, there was that half-man and half-woman. They didn't bill him/her as a hermaphrodite. People wouldn't have known what that was and would have been afraid of catching it. The barker emphasized that Saskatchewan law allowed him/her to appear on stage only if fully draped, so the only evidence to be seen of his/her condition was a bearded half-face and the rouged and lipsticked other side. The barker made sure that every twelve year old understood that "NO ONE UNDER SIXTEEN WOULD BE ADMITTED" and any under-aged rogues caught trying to sneak by might possibly be ejected.

Once we were inside, the M.C. announced that we were about to witness a presentation so astoundingly lascivious that our friends would never believe we'd actually seen it. To put an end to such doubt, he said, genuine photographs, unretouched, uncensored, and wallet-sized, were available, here and now, only, at a mere fifteen cents—two for a quarter. These actual photographs would show him/her undraped, hiding nothing, exactly as he/she was about to be revealed as soon as we passed through the curtain into his/her private chamber.

Well, the picture was in a sealed envelope, so you couldn't see it until you got out of there, but it certainly was a smudgy-looking print of what we saw—someone showing a bared chest with a bit of hair and a male nipple on one side, and a one-cup brassiere covering what looked like the shape of a small balloon on the other.

In another tent were the pygmies from wildest Africa. These turned out to be a little black woman and man, probably midgets. They sat in small chairs, looking bored, until given the cue to perform. The woman got up then and bent over with her rear end sticking out to show us a fuzzy little tail protruding from the back of her dress. The man's performance consisted of hollering "boolegga, boolegga, boolegga" when asked where he could find a drink. A five-minute educational lecture went along with this, which even all of us twelve-year-old sixteen year olds recognized as Pat Burns's purest baloney.

The biggest gyp, though, was the "Gold Diggers." There was a tent full of these little cranes in glass cases, each crane surrounded by stacks of nickles wrapped in colored cellophane, American silver dollars, heavy little toys, and big, awkward gewgaws. You put a nickle in the slot and then, if you wound the handle real fast, you could swivel the crane around to the prizes and, in theory, pick one up and carry it back to a chute that would deliver it into your greedy little paws. Well, it all worked just the way it was supposed to except that the only things small enough to be picked up in the jaws of the crane bucket were a single nickle or maybe a popcorn-prize engagement ring. If you did manage to lift one, then nine times out of ten it slipped out and fell back with the rest of the junk before it got to the chute. I usually had a whole dollar saved up to blow at the fair, and the first time we ever went, when I was nine or ten, the Gold Diggers cleaned me out in about ten minutes and left me with the rest of the afternoon to regret my folly. Fortunately, Dad paid for the grandstand seats, but it was a long, dry wait before the show could divert me away from my misery.

The misery was compounded by guilt because, as the afternoon wore on I suddenly realized that I had been a criminal as well as a fool, and yet it didn't seem to be all my fault. That morning, all of us kids had been dressed and jumping up and down with excitement and anticipation, and my dad had backed the car out of the garage, checked the oil and water, and kicked the tires. At that moment my mum decided she had to get the wash water ready for the next day.

The water from McCurdy's artesian well was hard, so before you could use it for laundry you had to soften it—a lengthy process. It required putting a washboilerful on the coal-and-wood range, dumping in a cupful of washing soda, and then slivering a cake of Pearl brand laundry soap into it with a paring knife. When you heated it the next morning, about two inches of grey scum rose to the top and you skimmed that off with a wooden spoon. The water was then fit to use in your washing machine. We all got busy and hauled the water to fill the washboiler, but then Mum realized she was out of soap, so she dug a fifty-cent piece out of her purse and sent me running to the Red and White Store. I got the soap alright, and forty cents change, and tore home as fast as I could go. Mum was so mad because everybody was nagging at her and I was so excited about the fair that we both clean forgot about that forty cents change. Well, you can guess the rest.

When we got to the midway I went on two of the rides and bought an ice cream cone—a nickle each because we always went on Children's Day—which left me with eighty-five cents out of my dollar. Suddenly I awoke to find myself in the Gold Diggers tent pushing nickles into one of the machines and on the verge of maneuvering a package of nickles close to the chute where I was certain the next attempt would drop it into my clutches. I changed a quarter and returned to work, but somehow that crane either flew right past the pack of nickles or just caught hold of the cellophane wrapper and let it slip away.

How could I quit now? If I did, I was out a whole thirty-five cents, while if I kept on, I might snag two of those nickle packs and be almost even. I changed another quarter, but before I could hurry back to my machine an outrageous thing happened. A big, tough-looking man opened up the back and pulled everything back to the starting place, so that I'd have to begin all over again to reap the bonanza offered by that machine. No way! I looked about and noticed someone leaving a machine halfway down the line, so I took possession and pushed in my starting nickle. It was a lucky machine. Before my quarter ran out I had snagged two nickles which, on a hunch, I immediately shoved back in the slot. My hunch was a good one, another nickle dropped out and went back into the coin slot.

Now I knew I was getting hot. Another quarter changed, two more nickles spent, and again a nickle dropped into the cup. I was crazy, I was nuts, I was on the verge of getting some of my money back. I reached into my pocket for another quarter. I'd lost count. Did I have one more, or two? But what the heck! I couldn't believe it, the pocket was empty. I tried to recall. Did I start out with three quarters or two? How many times had I gone to the change kiosk? It was a hopeless muddle, I couldn't think straight. In desperation the hope rose in me that I'd put my last quarter in the other side pocket. I searched it— nothing. Hopelessly I tried my hip pocket, but it was empty, as I knew it must be. I turned to leave when I suddenly realized I was wearing my Sunday pants, not my usual bib overalls, and there was a second hip pocket still offering a forlorn hope. Well, I couldn't believe it, I felt some kind of a coin there. I pulled it out—a nickle. How did that get in there? Could it be my Sunday School collection that I'd failed to put into the plate some time? No, that was impossible. I searched the pocket again and my heart leaped as I found two more coins, my missing quarter and a dime as well. None of it made sense, but I was past caring. Surely the tooth fairy or my guardian angel—or God—must have put them there.

So, against my better judgement and in spite of a still, small voice inside me saying "No," I felt certain it was all an omen, and I changed the whole thing to nickles and shot the wad. It was a long afternoon with not even one nickle left to buy a bottle of cream soda.

Next morning I woke to the hammering of the washing machine and I expected the worst. I found something to eat and wolfed it down, hoping to scoot out of the house before Mum caught up to me. But she came in and cleared away the dishes without a word, and when I came back at dinner time, there was again no hint of trouble. In the end, I guess she just never did remember about her change from the fifty cents and I never got the nerve up to tell her—not until I was fifty years old, and by that time I don't think she could understand what I was telling her any more.

Hey, Ma,
there's nothin' to do

But not only were there fairs; there were all kinds of other events with the same electrified atmosphere urging an unfamiliar and therefore urgent sense of irresponsibility. The most fairlike was a sports day or ball tournament, or even in special circumstances, a single ball game. Then there were the barnstormers skimming between barbwire fences and telephone lines to land their flimsy biplanes in pastures or summerfallow fields and begin taking up the well-heeled yokels at five bucks a pop for a ten-minute spin. And there were ninety-cent return adventures to Saskatoon on the eleven o'clock train that permitted five solid hours of debauchery on 21st Street beginning with a foot-long hot dog at Woolworth's, a bag of toasted coconut marshmallows at Kresge's, and ending way down past the cenotaph at Eaton's department store where we marveled at the opulence and were stunned to think that city people possessed the wealth to go in and select from it any time they wanted. Profligacy during those delicious times could be limited only by the utmost avail of one's purse.

On one excursion I bought my first suit of clothes: blue pinstripe stuff with vest and two pairs of long pants – $12.95 at Eaton's. And being old enough for long pants, I soon saved up and got my twenty-two rifle, a Ranger bolt action single shot – $4.95, brand new.

Just before we moved to Laura in 1926 the Orangemen had a big

July 12th celebration there with Orange Lodges from as far away as Outlook and Borden on parade. Gibson Photo came out all the way from Saskatoon with their new panoramic camera to take a picture of the assembly as they formed up ready to march. You can see a copy of the picture in the North Battleford Museum, and it shows both sides of town, the covered rink just under construction, the two-roomed elementary school, the church, the Imperial Lumber Yard, Pool and Quaker Oats elevators, fire hall, Grain Growers' Hall, F. E. Neal General Store, poolroom and barbershop, blacksmith's . . . Heck! you could go on. It was quite a town, you bet! Say, there's even the shack where the grass widow was said to make a living bootlegging strong drink for sure, and maybe other favors on occasion.

The people took the Orange Lodge pretty seriously, too, although they didn't seem to go in too much for the extremes, like the jingoism and the religious intolerance. Oh, they believed in it alright. Some, they said, even joined the K.K.K. They just never worked up the energy to get excited about it. You can tell that by the guy on the horse. It's a black one.

Anyway, most everybody was experiencing an unusually pleasant streak of prosperity and they found it pretty hard to get mad about anything for very long. You can see at least fifty-eight cars in that photo and there must have been a lot more parked out of sight along the main street on the south side of the tracks. And dressed up? Say, there's enough straw skimmers and sleeve garters to outfit a couple of dozen barbershop quartets.

I suppose most of the folks in that picture went up when the barnstormer came. We kids were all out in the school grounds for morning recess when somebody heard the drone of his engine and we all stopped, gawping upward, to be thrilled by the sight of a little two-seater biplane trundling low over the town, making a big, sweeping turn and then dropping down low over the school grounds and disappearing somewhere behind the grain elevators.

All the kids except me and my sister flew out the gates and along the streets and shortcuts, but we two, and the teacher, knew we'd catch it if we followed. At the edge of town they found the pilot just taking off from a summerfallow field with his first two thrill-seekers squeezed into the open air passenger space behind his cockpit. The poor teacher probably wanted to be there as much as we did but she couldn't get away with it either, so the three of us put in the day messing about at something until nearly three-thirty when she figured nobody would notice if we left.

Business must have been good. The plane stayed most of the next day, still jumping into the air every ten or fifteen minutes and swooping in low on return so that it swished through the gap between the telephone wires and the pagewire fence and scared people out of any notion of complaining at the brevity of five bucks worth of air travel.

Other planes came along in days to come but the thrill had already gone out of it. After those first two days of delicious abandon no more could be wrung from the experience. There was nothing to do now but to act blasé. When you've seen one airplane, you've seen 'em all!

Well, no, there was still one kind of airplane that sent us into a tizzy. It was the kind that came over, high up, and chucked out a bunch of advertising pamphlets. Kids ran for miles to get one of those. "Wildfire Coal from Drumheller" they usually said, which didn't really need to be advertised because after all, who would be dumb enough to face the coming freezeup without having ordered up ten tons of it for the drayman to dump down the cellar hole before the snow covered it in?

We used to get to Pike Lake three or four times a summer. There was the big sports day, the Sunday School picnic, and usually delivering or bringing home the girls from CGIT camp. Ice cream for these affairs came out on the train from Saskatoon in a tall tinned cylinder that held about four gallons. The cylinder was packed into a padded canvas bag with a padded, hinged lid. The four-inch padding usually kept the ice cream frozen pretty good until midafternoon if the weather wasn't too hot, but by three or so you'd have to pour it into paper cups to get rid of it.

Once the berries got ripe somebody in Laura used to organize whatever trucks and cars they could get. Then they'd load up buckets and boxes and cream cans and rain barrels – and pickers – and the whole town would spend a day filling everything with juicy, ripe saskatoons. Us little kids mostly picked into a syrup pail hung onto a shirt button and we usually ate as much as we picked. But it was a serious business for anyone half-grown-up, and by supper time they'd have hundreds of pounds of berries to be shared out when they got back to Laura. Every picker got enough to keep the wife busy all next day putting them up in jars for the winter's supply of fruit, even keeping out enough to provide fresh berries with sugar sprinkled on top and a dollop of cream for three or four suppers.

After that there were still the glossy red pincherries for jelly to put on your breakfast toast, and finally, fat, black chokecherries for wine and jelly and pancake syrup. People sure knew how to live high on the hog, and the canned stuff in the general store and the Red and White would collect a lot of dust before anyone would empty out their last quart sealer of wild fruit and be forced to buy it.

Saturdays most kids had chores of some kind to do: hauling wood and water for bath night, shovelling snow, cleaning out the fowl house, washing the windows, or weeding the garden. If we got done early enough we'd usually hang out on the steps of the general store in summer or in the barbershop once it got too cold. The farmers usually started to arrive about noon and we'd watch them coming in with their buggies and grain wagons and rattletrap cars in summer, or with sleighs and dog-boxes once the snow flew. You could learn a lot of stuff on Saturday afternoons, mostly dirty stories, but sometimes other things, some of them worth knowing. For example, there was this team of drivers that were always tied to the telephone pole halfway up between the general store and the hotel. They were real high steppers and pretty lively and unless you knew about horse's teeth you would have a hard time to tell which was the old one and which was young. To find out, you take a piece of straw and get down and touch the animal just behind a front fetlock. A young one will feel it and lift its hoof, but an old one will just continue to stand there paying no attention, unless it decides to kick your brains out.

There was one place just along the same stretch of board sidewalk where it was raised up over a hollow leaving enough space for a fairly large boy to crawl underneath and look up through the cracks. If you didn't get caught, you could learn quite a lot as the farm ladies strolled over to the hotel for an ice cream float after they'd dropped off their butter and eggs and put in their grocery order at the store. You'd learn a fair bit, too, if you did get caught.

Sundays, regardless of religious persuasion, we all went to Sunday School at the United Church, which was the only one in town. Most of our parents took advantage of that to have an hour alone without kids in the way. Then when we got home there'd usually be a big Sunday dinner waiting, with roast beef and Yorkshire pudding or leg of pork with the skin cut to make strips of crackling or a couple of roosters from the family flock or maybe a goose or a turkey. There'd be potatoes and lashings of gravy, boiled cabbage and turnips, carrots and parsnips, green peas or beans, homemade cranberry or apple sauce, horseradish, pickles, and sage and onion stuffing if we had poultry. And no matter how we stuffed ourselves there was always dessert, usually fruit pie or pumpkin pie with whipped cream, but sometimes we got creamy rice pudding with lots of raisins or tapioca or duff shot through with chunks of dates and covered in sweet white sauce.

After we'd cleared away, my dad would usually get the car out if the roads were open and we'd go to Kinley to swim in one of the spots on Eagle Creek or to visit friends, or we'd just spend a pleasant day driving around with the side curtains removed and sometimes with the top and the windshield down as well. But we nearly always got home early because we couldn't miss Fred Allen, Jack Benny, Edgar Bergen and Charley McCarthy, and Amos 'n Andy on Sunday night radio.

Deep woods,
sparkling waters

When I was a little kid somebody at Kinley brought a black bear cub from the hills. I don't know how it came to be tethered up on a chain beside Joe Tate's store for a while, but everybody came and had a look at it. Somebody told me it was sent to Saskatoon and ended up at the fairgrounds there. Anyway, I remember seeing a bear there, and it seems to me it was stuck in a sort of pit with an iron cage over the top. It was a pretty small place for a grown bear, and I remember feeling only pity when I saw it. But then there were lots more where it came from.

Another animal people were always chaining up was coyotes. There were lots of coyotes. Almost any night, especially in winter when sound travels, you'd hear a few coyotes singing out in a field nearby where they'd find a little hill for a platform. People shot coyotes whenever they could because they were chicken killers. And, anyway, their hides were worth something. Every spring somebody would find a den and dig up the pups and try to raise them till fall to make a few dollars but they never seemed to succeed. Either somebody's dog would get them or they'd escape, or they'd just die for some reason. There were always lots of stories about coyotes. They were about the smartest animals we knew and we admired them for that.

There was a farmer that lived south of Laura near the sand hills. I think his name was Alan Hill. He could never keep a dog. He said as soon as he got one the coyotes would find out, and one or two of them would get up on a mound back of the farmyard and yip and yap until the dog decided to teach them who was boss. Of course as soon as Rover or Buster or Sport reached the top of the rise, a dozen more coyotes would appear from the other side and tear him to bits.

Another farmer lived closer to town where coyotes were not usually seen. But one morning he got up and went out through the back porch to do the chores and there's a great big dog coyote standing right in the middle of the yard like he owned the place. The farmer's farm collie was right behind him, having been sleeping the night on some potato sacks in the corner, and as soon as he spotted that coyote, away he went after him like a tornado. Out the yard they went and down the half-mile lane to the pasture with the old collie gaining until he was almost nose to tail with that chicken thief. And then at the end of the lane that coyote turned in his tracks, surprising old Shep so he went ass over teakettle, rolled a few times in a cloud of dust, and then got chased all the way back up into the farmer's back porch. Then ol' coyote just stood there in the yard laughing his head off. That's another thing you admire about a coyote—he's got a real sense of humor.

Elevator repair crews came every summer for a few days to knock together some new wooden spouts or do some other minor maintenance jobs. Then one summer they came to dress up the elevator with a layer of new cladding and paint it—a three- or four-week job.

They were all Swedes and Norwegians with names like Olson, Svenson, Tolefson, or Nimmo, and they all seemed to have those hilarious-sounding Scandinavian accents that featured the same long vowels and rising inflections that were a mainstay of a lot of vaudeville comedians of the time. We called them "Scandihoovians," but it wasn't meant as a put-down. We thought they were wonderful, funny, carefree, and fearless. They rigged up ropes and scaffolds which they slid down and swung on through the air like circus high flyers, and they never seemed to stop yelling and singing and exuberantly horsing around. "Ole, Ole, Ole Olson, Yon Yonson, Pete Peterson," one of them always shouted as he stepped out the cupola window and slid down the sloping roof to a scaffold hanging somewhere down the side where they were nailing or painting.

These guys all lived up around Mont Nebo during the winters. I think they did a bit of farming up there when they could, but all winter they seemed to just hole up there until spring, ski jumping down the high slide they had built out of slabs and poles on a hill at one end of a lake. They'd come shooting off the bottom end to fly over a road, a shoreline of evergreens, and out onto the ice which they covered with straw to cushion the landings. One of them, Ole Tolefson, was their champion. His eyesight was weak, so he wore thick glasses, and the others told us that when he jumped, they would all stand near the bottom of the slide and yell, "Yump, Ole," when he reached the take-off mark.

For a couple of years in the thirties we had taken a week or so's holiday at a place on Long Lake (Last Mountain Lake) because I guess my dad still had nostalgic feelings about it from when he first arrived near there from England. But the fishing was getting pretty poor and other than swimming there wasn't anything else to do because the shore was just prairie infested with big, flying grasshoppers. So my dad was pretty receptive to the stories these repair crews told him about Mont Nebo, and finally, one summer, we went up there.

I don't know the name of the lake, so far as I knew it didn't have a name. But the place was as good as they said, in every way. The water was a bit icy, but after you ducked under it a few times you adjusted, and it was really refreshing during the hot afternoons. And it was loaded with fish. They were only jacks (pike), but they were the good, northern ones, not like the ones from the prairie sloughs that taste like mud.

There was a small, homemade rowboat that we rented, and a log barn with hay in the loft for us kids to sleep in. My dad had fixed the seats of our '29 Plymouth so you could lay the backs down to make a bed in the car for the adults. The lake was small enough that a good walker could go all the way round it in an afternoon and stop off at the far end to inspect the bare ski slide, or climb up it to look for miles over the evergreen forest and the lake. We'd take the little dog along that belonged to the owner of the barn, and he'd go crazy chasing the groundhogs all over the ski jump hill. I'd never seen groundhogs before, but the dog never caught one so I could see it up close.

The boat we were renting seemed to be the only one on the lake and was probably considered sort of a community resource because one day an old guy came along wanting to use it to catch a few fish. There was just me and my young brother and my dad—the girls and Mum had stayed home. And we had one of the farmers from Laura along with us who was a keen fisherman and good sport. Whenever we went fishing the fish just about jumped into the boat before you could get your trolling line halfway out, so he used to always chuck all the small ones back over the side. The old guy had brought along two gunnysacks to carry home his fish so he welcomed the company of the farmer, expecting to increase his catch.

It was a hot, lazy kind of afternoon and my brother and I sat down on the shore to watch. The two men rowed smartly out about halfway down to the far end and over along the left-hand shoreline where we'd found the fishing to be best. Then they let the boat drift, and we could see the movement as they cast their plugs and spinners on about ten feet of line tied to willow poles cut from the bush.

After about a half-hour we noticed that there seemed to be some unusually vigorous activity occurring in the boat, and then someone began rowing fast back in our direction. Something had obviously gone wrong. The oarsman was putting his back into it with all his energy, and the boat seemed to be riding lower in the water than we remembered.

As soon as they reached the shallows the old guy jumped out with water still chest deep and came plowing ashore, dragging the boat by the painter, with the farmer sitting in the stern obviously mad as a frustrated schoolteacher, and with water and dead fish sloshing around up to his calves.

We kids went and helped the old guy drag the boat up on the bank, and we scaled and gutted some of the fish for him. The farmer took off up to the car to dump the water out of his boots and hang his wet socks up on a bush to dry. When we were finished the old guy packed his two gunnysacks with fish and staggered away up a trail through the trees carrying a sack over each shoulder. He must have had more than a hundred pounds of jackfish.

What happened, we found out later when the farmer had cooled down a bit, was that within a few minutes they had caught so many fish that he didn't believe the old guy could use so many, so he chucked a few of the small ones back into the water. The old guy didn't like that, and when he caught the farmer doing it again, he started stomping the heads of the remaining fish so he'd have to stop. What he hadn't reckoned on was that the boards on the bottom of the boat started pulling away, and before he knew it, water was coming in faster than they could bail it out.

So we borrowed a hammer and managed to nail the boards back till the leaks were manageable, and the next day we had a good laugh about it all.

I'd like to go back to Mont Nebo and fish in that lake again, but I don't suppose I could find it now. And if I did find it, it'd probably be surrounded by campers and be half-full of plastic bags, rusty tin cans, and empty bottles, and there'd be one or two dead suckers floating in it belly up.

"Where're ya goin'?"
"Goin' to the rink"

That rink the Laura folks were building in 1926 turned out to be really something! Shares were sold, and everybody pitched in with volunteer labor between seeding and harvest. When they were done they had a round-roofed frame building covering a full-sized hockey rink with eight or ten tiers of seats along one side, and a vestibule with home team and visitors' dressing rooms at one end. There was a balcony above the dressing rooms, where they put the music machine for the skating, and where any overflow from the seats could stand and watch the games or the midwinter carnival. There was a lean-to all down the west side behind the seats, and under that were two sheets of curling ice separated from the rest by a wooden walk running back to the engine room. Along the walk was a rail that you could lean on while you kibitzed games. Or if it was real cold you could warm up in the men's or ladies' dressing rooms at the north end of the lean-to.

Once it got cold enough to put down ice the rink provided a weekly hockey game of some kind, curling for the adults every night, public skating three evenings and Saturday afternoon, and a midwinter carnival. But we kids never had to wait for that. By Halloween the ice would be thick enough on the sloughs and in the railway ditches to hold up us hockey-playing fools if we didn't all jump up and down in one place too much. And, anyway, when we did, the water was never much more than knee deep. So we mostly spent the winter weekdays after school and Saturday on McCurdy's Slough. It was a unique slough because, being fed under the ice by an artesian well, the water would burst out periodically and flood a whole new area. As soon as that froze we'd abandon our old location and bring our prairie rocks that we used for curling or for goal posts and our supply of burnables, mostly old tires, to the new one. A must at any of our macho gatherings, whether winter or summer, was a bonfire. Wood was scarce on the prairie and so we mostly relied on old tires for fuel. By the time our Saturday night baths rolled around I expect we must have been, as the saying went, "high enough to stink a dog off a gut wagon."

One spring we'd had a fair bit of snow and then we got an unusually mild chinook that turned all the snow to water that ran into the low places and then froze into perfect smoothness after the wind stopped blowing. The "Big Slough" north of the elevators flooded over and burst over two road allowances to make a magical skating surface nearly two miles long and half a mile wide at its widest. For ten days or so, every evening saw almost all the skate-owners within miles out on that marvellous expanse, gliding along in the semidarkness, alone or paired up with a girl, and trying to slip unnoticed to a lonely spot where they could try some fancy swoops and arabesques. No, we didn't try anything fancy with the girls; we didn't think they would have stood for it.

On the Saturday of that big spring chinook and freezeup, some of the kids skated to the farthest end of that slough. They jumped the foot or so of pagewire fence sticking up out of the ice where the road was flooded over and carried on another quarter mile right to the shoreline. While they were resting for the return they noticed that there were a lot of potholes in sight and close enough together that they decided to see how far they could go, skating the potholes and walking the few yards between. They ended up going clear to Delisle, about ten miles away by the course they took, and didn't get back until midafternoon.

Besides all that stuff there was to do in the winter, there was lots more. Some of us hunted jackrabbits and skinned them, and a few trapped weasels. When the ninety-cent excursion to Saskatoon came up we'd bundle up the skins in a big piece of brown paper saved from one of the Christmas T. Eaton parcels and sell them at St. Louis Hide and Fur right across from the station on First Avenue. Rabbits brought a dime for the best ones, and a nice, prime weasel as much as a dollar thirty-five, so the ten or twelve Saturdays spent enjoying yourself out in the snow at twenty below returned a nice profit. It was enough to pay for your ticket, a foot-long hot dog for lunch, and three or four boxes of twenty-two short cartridges at two bits apiece. And there'd be enough left for a nickle game of eight-ball at the poolroom pretty near any night you wanted until the mud dried up in the spring.

We boys all expected to grow up to play for the Maple Leafs, or for one of the other teams if we couldn't make the Leafs. Pat Gallagher, the CNR agent, usually coached kids' hockey on Saturday mornings. We'd turn out at nine-thirty with our skates and shin pads if we had them, or if we didn't, we used half an expired catalogue held over each shin with elastic bands cut from an old tire tube. Our hockey sticks were usually patched up discards from the adult team, spliced together and wrapped with half a roll of friction tape.

Pat generally just let us play shinny and tried to teach us a few of the rules, but one year a new agent came to run the Searle elevator just before they closed it down because there were no crops during the Dirty Thirties. He was a great fan of Charles Atlas, who advertised in all the ten-cent pulp magazines. Atlas was the guy who, as a ninety-seven pound weakling, got sand kicked into his face when he took his best girl to the beach. He sold a set of books that told you how to develop your body by the methods he'd used before he returned to the beach to humiliate that bully and win the devotion of every female in sight. The Searle agent had all the books at home and he'd come every Saturday at the end of practice and teach us another exercise of "Dynamic Tension." After that we all decided to become another "World's Most Perfectly Developed Man" and THEN to play for the Maple Leafs. By spring I could do push-ups away past a hundred until I got bored with them and switched to another "tension" maneuver.

We kids never had any outside competition because nobody could afford train fare to go to the next town as a team, and nobody would have spent good money to watch us. There weren't any roads open in winter and if there had been nobody would have gone to all the trouble of trying to start up a car just for that. But for the men's team it was a different story. Sometimes on weekends the Broadway Merchants' hockey team would come out all the way from Saskatoon on the evening train to play our guys, and people billeted them over until they left again the next morning.

Our guys were a pretty classy hockey team with stars like Les Miller and the Wylie boys, Ron Thompson, Shorty Rogers, Scoop Rogers, Mick and Lloyd Miller . . . One year they even got into the late games of the Intermediate League playoffs and when the roads went to mud in an early spring thaw, their opponents, Eston, hired a plane to fly up and land them in a field near our house. It was rumored that a five-hundred-dollar bet was riding on that game.

That rink even attracted hockey stars like Peggy O'Neill and Clint Smith who came out one Saturday with the Saskatoon Wesleys for an afternoon game. They went on to become stand outs playing in the NHL.

And there was the famous case of the Delisle Tigers the year during the Depression when Jack and Roy and Scoop Bentley couldn't make a living in the American West Coast League so they stayed home and played in the Saskatchewan Intermediate League. Besides the three oldest boys, who were seasoned pros, Reg and Doug and Max joined in, even though Doug was only about sixteen and Max was my age, fourteen. I think a brother-in-law played goal and there were some of the other pretty nifty hockey players around Delisle making up an unbeatable team. Apparently, after they won the Intermediate League Championship, somebody discovered an obscure rule that said the Intermediate League champs could challenge the champions of the Senior League if they wanted, so of course these guys did just that.

The Senior League champions that year were the vaunted Saskatoon Quakers. The previous year they had gone to Europe and won the World Crown, as the Canadians always used to do. They were highly insulted at the indignity of the small-town challenge, and they embarked on the series with a pretty disdainful attitude and considerable bad grace. Well, you can guess the result.

Because Delisle only had an outdoor rink they arranged to play their home games at Laura, and even though tickets went at thirty-five cents instead of the usual fifteen, the rink was busting at the seams. I saw one of the games. The eight tiers of seats were jammed. Up in the balcony more fans stood three deep against the fragile two-by-four rail, and some daredevil youths climbed up into the rafters and clung there risking a twenty-foot drop to the ice where the sweating players rushed end to end, crashing into the boards like broncos full of loco weed.

What struck me, and I still remember, was the way those Bentley boys could skate. They never looked back. They always faced the other guys' net. If they had to retreat they skated backward and they moved only in high gear either direction.

It was exhilarating, it was glorious. There's nothing today to match it. No Gretzky ever performed to the kind of enthusiasm we fans displayed, and he never will. So it was no surprise that Reg and Doug and Max all went on to the Blackhawks of the NHL, where Doug and Max, along with Billy Mosienko of Winnipeg became the "Pony Line," one of the all-time great goal-scoring trios.

Monday, Wednesday, and Friday (if there was no game), there was public skating which was mainly the young lads skating each of the town girls in turn cross-handed to the 78 rpm records played through the loud speaker. Pretty tame stuff, but then once a year there was the monster midwinter carnival bringing everybody in from the farms around as well as sleigh loads from Donavon, Delisle, and Tessier making their own roads across the drifted fields. We kids would be busy for weeks before, devising and sewing up costumes out of flour sacks, burlap, and any other odds and ends we could find. There were prizes donated by the local merchants as well as by Eaton's and Simpson's and even the Army and Navy Stores for prettiest costumes, comedy acts, most inventive, and so on.

There were skating races, figures, elegant pairs – something for everybody. One year they brought speed skaters out from the city and when we saw them swooping along on their fancy, long blades we knew they weren't a patch on our guys from the hockey team who challenged them. Heck, our guys would pass them the way the Thompson family drove their Hackney team past everybody on their way to church Sunday mornings.

But something happened. We couldn't believe it. Our guys shot away from the start just the way we knew they would: legs pumping like the drivers on a fast steam locomotive, heads down, sprays of ice chips glittering up in the electric light. Then, halfway round the first lap, those sissies, skating with one arm behind them and swinging the other one like a mule's tail in fly time, were catching up and going by. One by one, on the straightaway, they glided into the lead and by halfway through the second lap the last of our guys dropped out, beaten and humiliated. Well, we never invited them guys back again!

Oh, Oh!
It's forty below

Most of our parents, having emigrated from more moderate climates, found our prairie winters a bit much. Blizzards, forty below, frozen water pumps, and paths to be shovelled were bad enough. Finding the money for a cellarful of coal, extra coal oil for the lamps, new batteries for the radio, plus new felt boots and rubbers, long underwear, and overcoats for half the members of the family was a daunting prospect every fall. But for us kids it was all just normal. If we got penned in by a big blizzard we just waited it out in a nice, warm house full of the aroma of fresh-baked bread. If they shut down the school we just hoped it would last.

But winter wasn't all blizzards. Mostly, winter was pleasantly cold and if we were lucky there'd be snow with drifts big enough to tunnel into or to cut into blocks for building forts and igloos.

The land around Laura was pretty flat, but for a couple of miles to the west, there was a rise that took the CNR through a cut that was maybe ten feet deep at its deepest. About 1932 a big storm blew the cut full of snow and a long freight train rammed into it in the night with the blizzard at its height. The big steam engine almost bulled its way through, but not quite, and once it lost momentum it couldn't move either forward or back.

I don't know how long the crew stayed with the train, but somebody must have got out and walked the mile and a half into town to get a message stopping the morning passenger train from Kindersley. By morning very little of it could be seen any more sticking out of the drifts. Snowplows were sent out to both ends of the blockage but couldn't do anything with that freight train stuck in the middle of it all.

It became a temporary bonanza for the locals. Farmers were hired with their sleighs to load up passengers and carry them around to trains sent out from Kindersley or Saskatoon on the other side. Then as many men as could wield a shovel were put to digging out the freight cars at each end of the cut so that an engine could tow them out to the sidings at Laura and Tessier. We kids went out, alternately climbing up the hard, driven snowbanks and sinking waist deep in the sheltered places. When we reached the top all we could see was solid snow with occasional breaks where the tarred roofs and catwalks of boxcars showed level with the surface, indicating here and there where the train lay buried. It took nearly two weeks before the last car was shovelled free and the snowplows could clear out the remaining loose snow and tumbled chunks to restore service. After that, every time a bit of wind came up, a plow had to be sent through to clear out more drifting snow until finally a warm March chinook melted the surface and it froze to a hard crust.

A few years later we'd just settled down into our high school desks when there was the frantic whistle of a train nearby followed by a jolting, tearing crash that shook the foundations. It was one of those normally silent mornings when the thirty-five-below air hangs balefully, sparkling with ice crystals.

Our teacher told us to wait while he dashed out, without his coat or hat, to check it out. He was gone for a longish time and a few of the bigger louts were putting on their coats to follow when he returned to declare a half-hour recess so that we could all go and have a look at the train wreck right in the middle of town.

It was reported that the way-freight from Kindersley had pulled into town and, as usual, the crew hopped over to the general store to buy country butter and eggs. While they were occupied with that another freight came down the western slope behind them, found its brakes less than adequate on the frosty rails, and plowed into the unmanned way-freight, smashing through the caboose, a carload of coal, and two or three cars of oats and wheat, and then the engine rolled over on its side and lay there steaming. It looked exactly like a slow motion scene from a Hollywood movie, people said.

The way-freight crew with the help of some townsmen rushed to drag the engineer free from his overturned engine. He was relatively unhurt, and it was later discovered that he'd ordered the fireman to jump just before impact, so he was alright. The whole pileup occurred just clear of the station and most of the wreckage was clear of the siding track so that it was an easy matter to rig a temporary bypass. If it hadn't been for the weather, which didn't let up for three weeks or more, the whole thing might have been looked upon as another interesting and lucrative bit of CNR-hosted good fortune. But as it was, the men who got jobs cleaning up the debris were heartily pleased when it was all over and they could haul their carcasses back to the warm office of the town garage and resume their seats on the busted chairs and empty nail kegs around the Smear game table.

At school in Laura during winter there wasn't a heck of a lot for the farm kids to do at noon hour. They checked their horses in the barn and dumped the oat bundle from under their sleigh seat into the mangers, and then they came back out of the cold to open up their lard pails and swallow their jam sandwiches in the overheated classroom. Usually somebody sort of kept an eye out for the return of the teachers, who went back to the boarding house for a hot dinner. Why not? They were paying for it—twenty bucks a month!

After the old Grain Growers' Hall was converted to a one-roomed high school, the renovated building was equipped with the latest school paraphernalia, a Waterman-Waterbury circulating heater and a genuine chemistry laboratory.

The lab was housed in a large, home-built table which had a top made of four wide boards about twelve feet long. The outer two boards were fixed, and the middle two could be lifted off to reveal a compartment half-full of alcohol lamps, iron stands, beakers, and test tubes.

One noon hour an empty ink bottle got left on the table and someone swooshed it from one end to the other the way a western barman swooshed a schooner of beer along to a thirsty cowpoke at the far end of the bar. Somebody else used a stick of chalk to draw a target to aim for and a game developed with a half-dozen players and as many bottles, and it got so exciting that the teacher walked into the middle of it before he was noticed.

"Curling, eh?" he commented. Then he took off his coat and went to his desk to get ready for the afternoon's work.

The players returned their ink bottles to their desks and sat down expecting trouble. "Not a great idea, is it?" the teacher said. "Next thing a bottle will get broken and you'll have ink and broken glass all over everything. Anyway, it's not a very satisfactory game because not enough people can play. What you should do is get hold of some blocks of wood and curl up and down the aisles. You could have four or five games all going at once and even have a bonspiel."

Next morning the boys came in bringing up to a dozen nice, round poplar blocks they'd bucksawed off the family fuel supply. A day or two later the teacher came with a box of brass upholsterer's tacks and we found that if we put three of them into the bottom of each block they would curl just like real rocks on ice. It was so interesting that the town kids came back early to play, and we really did have a bonspiel, although there were no prizes. The games went on until well into spring and only stopped when most of the blocks dried out so much that they split.

So, as far as we kids could see, winter brought about as much good as bad. Still, there was one winter activity that had the potential to cause an agonizing death. When the red line of the thermometer shrank down nearly out of sight it was fun to stick your tongue on the knobs and hinges of a north-facing door when you lost interest in other indoor pursuits. It was a fairly innocuous pastime that provided a sense of daring but only the danger of a swollen tongue or a skinned lip. But it wasn't a great idea to try it outdoors.

My dad used to take a kettleful of boiling water out to thaw the ice in the chickens' drinking dish when the weather got real cold. One thirty-below Sunday afternoon he woke up from a snooze to realize he'd forgotten the chickens and it was already starting to get dark. So he pulled on his mackinaw and mitts and grabbed the kettle off the stove. He was just about to open the henhouse door when he thought he heard a strange, strangling cry nearby in the dusk. Then he saw that someone was bent over the galvanized iron shield that covered the anchor holding the last post of the powerline nearby. It was the neighbor's little girl, about eight. She'd stuck her tongue to the shield and had evidently been there, alone, for some time. By now her lips were also frozen down and there was considerable blood around them. Luckily the kettle had cooled a bit and he was able to melt her loose with the hot water without doing any more damage. The little girl's sore mouth healed up eventually without a scar, but it was pretty scary to think what might have been.

One other time the little three-year-old son of one of the elevator agents was found with his tongue stuck to the CNR rails. He'd been on his way to visit his dad. Luckily that day wasn't really all that cold, and I guess he hadn't been there long anyway, but it could have been a terrible tragedy. He was a real nice little kid. In the summertime he was always getting stuck in the gumbo mud and he'd just wait there until somebody came along and then he'd holler out, "Hey, I'm stuck!"

That same winter I once found him caught by the seat of his pants in a barbwire fence. He was just waiting there for somebody to come and unhook him, no panic, no tears. He'd probably been there a half-hour or more.

Winter cold was more of a challenge than a threat. We kids slept in the two upstairs rooms of the company house. The only heat in one bedroom came up through a stovepipe hole cut through the ceiling above the kitchen range. In the other, there was a similar hole above the Quebec heater in the living room below. On washdays the walls would accumulate a thick layer of frost, and we went to bed every night with hot water bottles, which we kicked out when they got cool and found frozen solid on the floor in the morning.

Often sleep would be disturbed by a herd of horses turned out to forage for themselves all winter by a farmer who'd run out of feed or didn't want the trouble of looking after them. They'd come around the house at night pawing through the snow to get the prairie grass that had been growing undisturbed all summer. Twenty or thirty hungry horses made a strange and scary racket. Next day you'd go out and find the snow plowed up as if some strange farm machine had been through preparing the landscape for some outlandish crop.

One winter night we woke up about midnight to a noise like thunder booming and rolling across the fields. It was eerie and threatening because there is no thunder with a winter storm. A warm chinook had been blowing false promises of spring all day, but then in the evening it switched to the northwest. The temperature plunged to thirty or forty below zero in a couple of hours and then the wind dropped to an ominous dead calm as we crept to our freezing beds. At first a thick, solid crust had formed over the miles of snow-covered fields. Then as the Arctic cold settled over the land the crust began to shrink and crack, sending a booming, rolling doomsday message across the fields and resounding through the heavy air. Just before we returned to sleep a train roared in from the east and its whistle split the night with a drawn-out shriek.

It was Saturday, and we woke up to find a gruesome scene in the center of town. The horses must have tried to take shelter from the terrible cold by bunching up on the tracks in the lee of one of the grain elevators. And now five lay dead where the speeding predawn freight had ripped through them and the fox farm man was there cutting them up before they froze solid to make meat for his silver foxes.

In the

sum, sum, summertime

A lot of the people around Kinley were from England and so they had a pretty strong cricket club until people lost interest. In the twenties we still used to drive over there from Laura in the Model T because my dad still played for Kinley, and they'd have a match most Saturdays. There were large crowds at the games, and during the break, everybody would surge up to the school where the ladies served sandwiches and lemonade and tea. We Macklon kids would stand around uneasily, noticing that Kinley kids stared at us and formed little whispering groups of critics because already we had become foreigners.

About the time that the cricket club folded, our best friends moved from Kinley to Juniata, so we didn't have much reason to go to Kinley any more.

We kept up the summer ritual of the twenty-fourth of May, though. For most of the Laura people the twenty-fourth was "the Queen's Birthday," but to us it was "Perdue Sports." We never missed it. It was one of the biggest and best baseball tournaments of the year, but for me, I mainly went for the ice cream and for two things they had in Perdue that we didn't have in Laura—a band and a movie theater.

It seems to me the band played all day in the sports grounds bandstand, but I guess they couldn't have had that much stamina. Anyway, they played loud and they played a lot of familiar stuff, and they had uniforms and everything. Listening to them gave people an excuse to sit down, which was nice for kids and the old folks. You got pretty tired wandering around in the spring sunshine. But it was more than just a rest for me. I was fascinated by the display of instruments. All the brasses were polished up like gold, and there were reeds and percussion instruments I'd never known to exist before. I wondered how you could get so many notes out of an instrument with only three keys, and how you kept such a flimsy-looking thing as a trombone from getting bent so it wouldn't slide any more. It seemed impossible to me that anybody could ever master all those complicated keys on a clarinet.

In the midafternoon we kids would wander down to the theater where they usually showed a great cowboy movie with lots of outlaws chasing stagecoaches or Indians chasing covered wagons. Somehow the coaches and wagons managed to outrun the bad guys even with their wheels turning backwards. What I liked best, though, were the cartoons they started off with. They were always about an old grandpappy guy with a long chin whisker that bobbed up and down when he talked. Of course he didn't really talk, because these were silent movies. The old guy ran a movie house, and he was always in trouble. His hand-cranked projector would get going either too fast or too slow, or he'd get the film in backwards or upside down and have the ship sailing across the screen under the ocean, or a burglar running backwards toward a bunch of backward-running cops. One cartoon used the same slightly naughty sight gag that, much later, became a mainstay of English comedian, Benny Hill's skits—the partially covered sign. In this one the old guy painted a sign on his double swinging door that said:

TEN   CENTS
WILD   WEST
WOMEN   HALF PRICE

Then he opened the right-hand door and put a brick against it and the crowds of men came a-runnin'.

At the height of the Dirty Thirties we couldn't afford to go to Perdue any more, but I did go once on my old bike. I rode up to Juniata the day before and stayed overnight with my friend. The next day the two of us rode to Kinley where we picked up another friend, the son of the cafe owner, and the three of us rode on to Perdue. It used to be great fun for me, riding long distances on the dirt roads, but it wasn't so great riding on the gravel highway, especially when a car went by and raised a suffocating cloud of dust. The dust would hang in the still, hot air in a cloud a half-mile long before it finally drifted off to settle over the sparse remains of the dried-out crops.

The three of us left Perdue about ten at night and rode back to Kinley where we separated to go to our homes. I had nineteen miles to go, but I always loved the excitement and sense of freedom that came from sliding through the darkness without a light, knowing every turn of the way and anticipating every bump or hollow. That night, as I pedalled easily along the correction line, I began to feel pretty thirsty, so when I came to Woodlawn School I wheeled through the gate to pump a cold drink from the well. I put one hand under the spout to drink from, while I worked the handle with the other. The water was cold, and I swallowed a quart or so before I was suddenly aware of an awful taste in my mouth and my throat and clear down to my stomach—dead gophers! The well must have been half-full of them. It took most of the next day before that taste disappeared, and I waited for a couple of weeks for signs of typhoid or bubonic plague or something to show, but nothing happened.

There used to be a place in the sand hills just west of Harris where somebody had dumped sand along the shore, and a few feet out into the water, of a muddy-bottomed slough. A ramshackle pavilion had been built and some kind of golf course laid out through the scrub. Its imaginative proprietor named it "Crystal Beach." They had illegal one-armed bandits in the pavilion that ate up nickles at an alarming rate and probably did more than anything to keep the place solvent, especially when the Depression hit. In its heyday, about 1930, some people had built cottages there and spent their vacations in them or rented them out. But although it was a nice enough, inexpensive place to spend a few days, a full two-week holiday must have been pretty boring. I once rode my bicycle there from Laura and spent the night with friends who had rented a cottage. But it wasn't worth the effort of fighting a headwind over the gravel road on an ancient, single-speed machine.

Travelling baseball teams showed up two or three times a summer to play against the locals, and people from all the towns around came to see them and make a day of it. Most popular was "The House of David," whose players were supposed to be members of some religious sect and wore their hair long and tied in a pony tail, and mostly grew beards. The other was "The Kansas City Colored Giants." A number of such teams used to come up to Canada from the States every summer and make some kind of precarious living from the gate receipts. There were some very good ball players, both white and black, on those teams, but the people came out to see them more because guys with long hair and beards and black guys were real strange-looking creatures and the locals could chuckle about their crazy differences from us normal people for weeks after.

The Colored Giants and the House of David and the others usually reserved playing against each other for the bigger places where the gate receipts might be expected to bring enough to give each team a decent share. My dad took me to see a game in Saskatoon when the tours were at their height, and the black guys trotted out that fabulous pitcher Satchel Paige for one inning. It was rumored that Satchel got paid a hundred bucks a game for this, but I doubt it. In fact, I'd be surprised if the gross gate came to that much. I was thrilled to see Satchel. He was all arms and legs and he looked too skinny to put any beef behind a throw, but he sure fooled me. He just stood up there on the mound and blew nine strikes past the batters, who mostly just stood there as if they hadn't seen the ball go by—they probably hadn't. But I didn't think a whole lot of the game. It seemed to me the batters just hit the ball right into the fielders' gloves. My dad said that was because of the good pitching, but I wasn't convinced.

What I remember best about the night, though, was what the black guys called a "pepper game." About halfway through the game there was a delay, that might have been contrived, and the whole team ran out into the infield and spent ten minutes or more just tossing balls and gloves and sometimes thin air back and forth at a blinding speed, and never in the direction you expected. Most of the time they kept a dozen or more objects flying around at once, and there was never a miss, although to me, it looked impossible to anticipate which direction a ball or glove or a hat might be coming at you. And all the time it continued, they kept up a laughing chatter as if they were having the time of their lives. It was wonderful. I now realize that is the mark of a great entertainer: to look as if what you are doing is being done for the first time and you can't believe how much fun you're having.

In the summer, we kids always played baseball as the game of choice, unless there were girls, and then we played "Board in the Hole." That was a game like cricket except you used any kind of bat and ball that was available, and you used three tin cans, one piled on top of two, for a wicket. In front of the wicket we dug a hollow, and the batter had to keep his bat tip in that "hole." If the wicket was knocked over by a thrown ball or kicked over by any player holding the ball while the bat was not grounded, the batter was out. That's why we called it "Board in the Hole." A bowler threw the ball underhand along the ground, and if you swung at it and missed and the cans went down, you were out. But if you hit the ball you could run to the opposite end of the pitch where there was another hole and another wicket. Getting your board in the hole at the opposite end before the cans went flying scored a run. If you hit the ball far enough you might run back again and score a second run, and so on. As long as nobody could knock over the cans while your board was out of the hole you stayed alive to continue batting, but there wasn't much point in just staying alive. You had to take some chances and try to score some runs. It was a pretty good game, especially when the Depression hit, because it could be played without any "bought" equipment at all.

At school, though, we played softball. Each family would bring a dime and the teacher would go to the hardware store and buy a softball. The bats seemed to last forever, but the balls always got softer and softer until finally the seam split open. Then one of us would take the remains home and sew it up with waxed store string. The centers were made of kapok which was wound with several layers of string, and after the leather cover had been sewn a half-dozen times, the kapok would start to disintegrate and leak out of the string. At that stage we would make a new core out of rags, rewind it with the string, and sew it up into the cover again. That way a ball bought in April would last right through to November, when hockey took over. There were no worries about a shortage of pucks because there were still lots of horses around.

They break a lot of bats in the ball games you see on television these days. Sometimes the bat splits and bloops the ball shallow for what they call a broken bat single, and sometimes the fat part of the bat goes flying into the stands, threatening to brain one of the fans. This amazes me because back at Laura our baseball team's equipment was brought to the diamond in a gunny sack and consisted of an old catcher's mitt, a belly pad, shin guards and mask, two grass-stained balls, and three bats.

Players, other than the catcher, brought their own gloves, and sometimes visiting teams forgot their equipment and used ours. The three bats lasted three or four years that I know of. One was heavy, one light, and the other was one that had been cracked, glued and dowelled back together, and then wrapped with friction tape. If anybody had broken one of those bats he'd probably have been pounded into the ground like a fence post with the other two.

The way to not break a bat is to hold it right. Players making two million dollars a year don't seem to know that now, but every kid around Laura knew. Bats are made of wood with a fairly coarse grain. As a tree grows it makes a new ring, or layer, of wood between the bark and the last year's layer. If you take a big tree and saw it up into baseball-bat-sized pieces, you end up with maybe a hundred or so billets, each containing about a dozen plies of wood from the various layers in the tree. When the bat maker is done with one he stamps a label on it so that, if you hold the bat with the label on top or bottom, you will hit the ball with the edges of the layers of grain. But if you hold the bat with the label to the front or back, you hit the ball flat on the layers. It's like the difference between hitting with the edge of a ruler and hitting with the flat face of it. It is much stronger from edge to edge.

Not only are you less likely to break a bat if you hold it with the label up, but the bat will flex less and should drive the ball farther.

You watch any of these big shot professionals today and you'll see they pick up the bat and start twirling it around like some smart-ass kid while they're on deck, and never even look at the label before they go to the plate. But Rudy York and Hank Greenberg must have known. I remember a game where between them they drove about two pailsful of balls out of the park, and not one broken bat.

Hey, diddledee dee,
a farmer I won't be

Even if there'd been no drought and the bottom hadn't dropped out of the market for farm products, I'd have never made a farmer. I don't know how the immigrants that came to the prairie from Europe and wherever learned how to farm here. Some homesteaders bought teams of fractious broncos in Regina and had to get the seller to harness them. Then when they reached their land they were afraid to take the harness off, partly through fear of the unruly horses, but often because they were afraid they'd never figure out how to put it back on. Barry Broadfoot's oral history book, *The Pioneer Years*, is full of such stories. He even tells of a man named Hanson, who fleeced fifteen to twenty newcomers at a time by running a farming school where greenhorns learned by following him around as his did the chores on his quarter section.

Years ago, I found a little, paper-bound book on the library shelf of a one-roomed country school. It was written by a man who'd settled down around Strasbourg, and he must have homesteaded there about the same time as my dad and the Smiths did, although he was from Sweden or Norway. He said that he came to Canada with his wife, and following the normal procedure, he picked out a homestead on the map in the Regina land office, bought a team and a wagon which he loaded up with supplies, and headed out to see what he'd got.

He didn't have a lot of trouble finding the surveyor's stakes, and he'd brought along plenty of groceries, so since the land looked good to him, he and his wife unloaded the wagon and dumped the wagon box onto the prairie grass upside down. She was to wait there, with the box for shelter, while he returned to Regina, with the horses hooked to the running gear, to register his homestead claim and buy a few more things they would need.

By the time he finished his business in Regina and completed the round trip with his horses a week or more had gone by. He got back some time in the afternoon and when he felt he was in the vicinity he was surprised, and then dismayed, to see no sign of his wagon box or his wife. He was certain they must be nearby but they just seemed to have vanished. By the time he had searched for an hour or more he was in a panic. He began to believe that all the assurances he'd received that his wife would be safe there alone must have been wrong, and that some wild animals or an Indian war party had carried her off. Still, he couldn't believe anyone could have taken the wagon box as well. It began to get dark, and he was driving up and down through the tall grass in desperation when he thought he heard someone calling. He stopped and listened and he heard it again, and this time he was sure. He called back, but he still saw no sign of them. Eventually, by moving in the direction of the calls, he got near enough to see his wife's head and shoulders amid the grass. He hadn't reckoned on grass that could grow so fast; the green painted wagon box had been almost lost in it.

And if he thought HE was frightened, I wonder what terror must have gone on in his poor wife's mind all that time. And she must have suffered a million mosquito bites.

But little credit seems to have been accorded women, and yet surely the prairies could never have been farmed without them. When I drive past one of the hundreds of caved-in farmsteads hemmed by the remnants of half-dead trees and sitting all alone, miles from anything, I think about the woman who came there, young and pretty and trusting her man. I see her carrying well water, slopping the pigs, scrabbling a few vegetables from a weedy garden patch, and milking the cows while her man chewed the fat with real human beings at the grocery store and hardware in the town she never saw, except when the elevators sometimes showed themselves shimmering in the mirage of a hot, summer day.

The first shack my own parents occupied was a single room somewhere down Lockwood way, and in winter one of them had to get up and light a fire in the wood stove to thaw the ice out of the kettle and warm the place enough to start the porridge.

During the bonanza days on the prairie I was too young to join the harvest crews. It took a lot of men each fall to cut the shoulder-high Marquis wheat, stook it up, and then haul it to the big, steam threshing outfit. On the threshing crew the two most important men were the steam engineer and the separator man who had to be up before everyone else. The engineer had to make steam and fill the oilers and grease the bearings. All day he watched for signs of impending breakdown or loss of power. Everything had to go while the sun shone. The separator man went out with the engineer at 4:00 A.M. to get his threshing machine ready. The leather lacings of a dozen or more flat drive belts had to be inspected and any worn laces replaced. The reservoirs that greased and oiled the bearings had to be filled, the shafts tested for wear, and the screens examined for damage. It wouldn't do to have grain lost out the straw blower, or chaff and weed seeds not separated from the grain. There was a water man keeping the steam boiler filled with water which he pumped by hand from the nearest slough, using a double-acting, hand-operated pump mounted on top of a wooden tank wagon. Another man with a team and hayrack dug straw out of the stack and drove it to the engine to fuel the fire-box. A half-dozen bundle wagons drove out from the separator in pairs to where two or three field pitchers helped load sheaves from the stooks until they were ten feet high on the bundle wagons (racks), and the drivers rushed back to maneuver their wild-eyed, frightened teams into position beside the noisy separator. Then the spike pitchers climbed aboard to help, so that two men from each side tossed bundles, headfirst, onto the feeder, furiously, as if there was a contest to see which driver could take off first, horses at the run, to reload. Two or three more men with teams pulling grain boxes hauled either forty or sixty bushels at a time into the farmyard granaries or straight to the elevators in town.

Back at the farm there was a cook boiling and frying and roasting and baking lashings of meat and spuds and gravy and peas and corn and carrots and cabbage and cauliflower, and then cakes and pies and big loaves of bread. A couple of cook's helpers picked and dug in the garden and podded and peeled and scraped and kneaded and then washed and scrubbed and carried and set and served. At noon one of them hitched up the democrat and loaded the noon lunch for the threshing crew out in the field. She took washtubs full of meat sandwiches or buns and fried chicken, boxes full of chocolate layer cakes, bushel baskets of apples and oranges, and cream cans full of hot coffee. She got to rest a few minutes while it all disappeared down the men's hungry throats, and then galloped the horses back to the barn, a long dust cloud floating above their track through the dry stubble, and joined in the preparation of supper.

When dusk fell, the engineer blew his whistle, and all the field hands trooped into the farmyard, unharnessed their horses and watered them, and gave them a brush. Then they came swarming into the cook car to be served the mountains of food and the gallons of coffee the women had waiting. And long after the men had rolled into their bunks, snoring and farting, contented as hogs in a straw stack, the women dried the last of the dishes, washed down the oilcloth table tops, swept up the floor, toted the garbage and the slops, and then set their alarm clocks for four and collapsed into their bunks.

There used to be two rhymes about threshing crews, just the men. I guess nobody had time to be aware of the women. The short one went:

> A fartin' horse will never tire,
> And a fartin' man is the man to hire.

The long one was:

> The separator man lay in the stack,
> And the engineer lay on the ground.
> The hobo pitched like a son of a bitch,
> And the wheels went round and round.

I think that was all the poetry that ever came out of it all, but there was a ton of material there. I guess the women were just too darned tired, and the men too vulgar and macho. It all makes one appreciate Sarah Binks, the Sweet Songstress of Saskatchewan, whose poetic career was so hilariously chronicled by University of Manitoba professor, Paul Hebert in his fictional biography, *Sarah Binks*. In spite of her distracting liaison with the John Deere salesman from Regina, Sarah poured out a veritable avalanche of verse to delight the readers of *The Horse Breeder's Gazette*, the editors of which once awarded her first prize in a poetry contest—a horse thermometer.

As for me, by the time I reached threshing-crew size, there was little or nothing to thresh. And what little there was paid a buck and a quarter a day.

I got a day's work in 1936 hauling grain from the last steam outfit around Laura. It belonged to Alf Miller and the engineer was Harry Rogers. Harry was handy with all the obsolete farm skills. He shoed horses, pounded out new edges on red-hot plowshares, shrunk steel tires back onto wooden wagon wheels, and joined broken steel parts back together with blacksmith's welds done in his forge. About that time he'd got into the almost full-time manufacture of horse-drawn Bennett wagons, out of the cars that people could no longer afford gas for.

The previous year I'd put in two or three days stooking, but the farmer didn't think I was fast enough, and I didn't ram the sheaves into the ground hard enough, so my stooks tended to fall over in a high wind.

But my final day of farming was pretty close to my final day, period. After I finished up hauling grain from the steamer, another farmer hired me to drive a hay rake. I went up and down where the rows of stooks had been picked up, to gather up any stray bits left on the ground. This farmer's horses had a lot of bronco blood in them, and they tended to spook, but the team of old mares I got seemed pretty slow and lethargic, although one of them had a pretty frisky young colt following at her side. I didn't know a lot about the fine points of horsemanship so I asked another guy for advice about how short to hitch the harness tugs. It was important to get that right. There was a long wooden pole attached to horse-drawn machinery that ran up between the horses, where it was held up by passing through a steel ring attached to a wooden cross-piece. The wooden cross-piece was called a neck-yoke and it was strapped at each end to the horses' collars. That way, when the horses changed direction, the machine was steered to follow them. The harness tugs had to be hooked up short enough to prevent the pole from slipping out of the neck-yoke ring when the horses took up the slack on a hard pull. I should have used my own judgement.

By late afternoon of the third day I had pretty well cleaned up the field, so the boss sent me to the yard to leave the rake and bring out a grain wagon to hold the last of the wheat from the thresher. The old mares thought it was an early night off, so they pricked up their ears and started up the trail at the trot.

The rake was an old dump rake that had a row of curved tines across the back which were curved to gather up hay and roll it into a roundish bundle. The bundle was released every now and then by a foot-pedal that engaged a mechanical ratchet device in one of the wheel hubs, and power-lifted the tines. There was also a lever you could use to raise the tines by hand, and there should have been a hook to hold the lever down and keep the tines raised while you travelled between jobs. But this rake was missing the hook, and so as I headed for the yard, I held the lever down with my foot.

We were stepping along at a pretty smart pace when we came to a bit of a dip. The old rake caught up to the horses' rear ends as we rolled down the slope, causing the pole to push into the neck-yoke ring, and pulling uncomfortably at the horses' collars. At the same time, the tugs drooped down because nothing was pulling on them for the moment.

But as the horses laid into their collars on the uphill side, they took up the slack with a sharp jerk, the tugs stretched out just enough to let the pole slip out of the neck-yoke ring. When the pole hit the rising ground it drove in like a javelin, the machine tried to somersault over it, and I was thrown between the horses. That released the lever holding up the tines of the rake.

The bronco blood took over. The old horses lunged, snapping off the wooden pole, and thundered off at the gallop with the colt prancing ahead, enjoying all the excitement. The toe of my shoe had caught in the angle of a steel brace, so I was on my back under the rake, being dragged through the stubble, and unable to do anything to save myself.

I did have the presence of mind to realize that if my foot ever came loose, I could be caught up by the tines and ripped to ribbons, so I reached back behind my head and pried the two tines as far apart as I could. Just as I did that, my shoe ripped across the instep letting my foot loose, and I managed to steer my upper body between two tines. One tine caught my belt and threw me clear, and then, about twenty feet ahead, the mares took either side of a telephone pole, bent the rake into a crescent, ripped the harness to bits, and charged through the farm gate and into the barn.

Of course it was all my own fault. Prairie kids were expected to know about horses and farm machines and all that stuff. They learned it by osmosis, you were dumped into it and it just sort of soaked through your grimy hide and found its way to your brain. But you see, that was what came of memorizing all that poetry in school. It tended to block up all your corpuscles and things and kept any sensible learning from getting through.

I got up, dug some of the dirt out of my eyes, and limped back to the thresher where I finished up the day shovelling wheat in the bin. That evening the farmer drove me back into town and reluctantly paid me the full three seventy-five. The next day my ankle was swelled up like a section of inner tube and aching like a rotten molar. But three or four days later the swelling started to go down, and there was only a strange, hard lump sticking out at the side. I figured I was lucky to be alive, and now, fifty-odd years later, I can't seem to find the lump any more, so I guess it's pretty well healed up.

Academia
for the macademia

Any Saskatchewan village could get a travelling library. It was a grey-painted wooden box with metal handles on the ends that opened up like a clamshell. Inside were about fifty books in a variety chosen and considered suitable for our small town populations by some government department in Regina. Usually one of the teachers took charge of the Laura box, shipping it on to the next town after a month or so, and receiving a replacement from the town in the opposite direction. In this way each town could have a half-dozen of these book collections every winter until they were all shipped back to Regina in the spring for reconditioning and updating.

Those books relieved a good deal of the monotony of prairie winters. Besides, at Laura, going over to the teacherage to exchange books gave us kids a chance to meet the teachers in a bit different atmosphere than at school. We always had two women teachers sharing a shanty of a teacherage and a male high school teacher/principal who boarded out.

So we'd walk timidly over to the teacherage on a Saturday and brush and stomp a bit to get rid of some of the snow, and then we'd knock on the door with our mittened knuckles. After a while one of the women would let us into the lean-to kitchen. She'd lead us past the coal range with the washtub on it full of snow being melted down for their Saturday night baths and into the freezing cold living room containing nothing much more than the library box set up on a couple of rickety chairs. I think we were allowed two books per person at one time, and while we pawed through the box to pick out two new ones the teacher would be leafing through our returns to make sure all the pages were still there and nobody had crayoned any art work onto the flyleaves. Those Regina people must have disinfected the books with something every year because they always smelled funny in a pleasant kind of a way.

We'd look for a new *Tarzan* or something by Mark Twain or a Gene Stratton Porter or a Clarence Mulford. Or if they were all out, or we'd already read them, we'd try something new—*Michael O'Halloran, Little Knight of the X-bar-B, Studs Lonigan* . . .

We'd usually tell the teachers about the books we'd enjoyed and they'd take the opportunity to ask us about what we were occupying ourselves with and we'd actually get quite friendly. It was amazing, especially because in school they never seemed friendly at all. I suppose it was hard for them to relax because they were expected, above all, to keep discipline, and that meant having the strap in a handy place and frequently taking it out for exercise.

Teachers usually got criticized and gossiped about whenever two or more of the villagers met. But they were usually safe in their thirty-five-dollar-a-month jobs as long as the kids came home with news of a strapping every once in a while and they put on a good Christmas concert. Folks didn't really hold it against them if their kids couldn't figure out how many cords of wood in a pile; or how far apart two trains would be at nine-fifteen if one left A heading for B at eight-ten travelling thirty-seven miles per hour, and the other left B heading for A at eight-thirty-seven travelling forty-two miles per hour and making one stop of three minutes and another of two; or if they failed to memorize all the verses of "The Wreck of The Hesperus." They realized all that was just junk you did in school and didn't matter a whoop in real life.

So the teachers seldom allowed themselves to appear even compassionate or forgiving, let alone friendly. It was only at recess that school was any fun, and for the few kids who were outcasts it must have been sheer hell all day and every day, week in and week out.

For one thing, the teachers all had their pets who monopolized their attention and basked in their praise. After all, teachers were usually either eighteen-year-old farm girls, strangers in town, starved, half-frozen, and lonely, or prematurely middle-aged, forbidding-looking rejects from the nubility pool, starved, half-frozen, and lonely. So who could blame them for latching on to the few among us who were handsome, reasonably sweet smelling, and compliant. Those of us who weren't were either barely tolerated or totally ignored, depending on our places, or the places of our families, in the community pecking order. I was a good student, usually top in the class, but I don't remember a teacher ever remarking on it. They frequently picked up on my many deficiencies, though, and harped on them to no end.

But I was lucky: I only got strapped six times in my school career and that was all in one year by a "strapping fool" who once strapped the kid who stuttered four times before the first recess. Later on we got a teacher of the prematurely middle-aged category whose forte was cracking you across the knuckles with the end of a four-foot wooden blackboard pointer. She used to do this to me whenever I put my books away because I had finished my work ahead of the rest. I found it very encouraging!

I remember in the junior grades at Laura a girl whose father lived on a farm four miles or so away. He was one of the misfits, but not with me, because he bought me a stick of horehound candy one Saturday afternoon in the Red and White Store. I don't know whether he had a wife to mother the girl, but he must have been very poor.

The girl's long woollen stockings always hung in bulging wrinkles at the top of high boots that buttoned up the side and were several decades passé. She might have had two homemade dresses cut from the same bolt of checkered gingham but always seemed to have the same attire. A homemade haircut, straight around just below the ears with straight bangs covering her forehead down past the eyebrows, was inflicted upon her coarse, black hair now and then, but otherwise she seemed completely uncared for. She was like a whipped dog, and although at home she may have been loved in an undemonstrative kind of way, she seemed to know her place lay at the bottom of the heap, and she accepted that.

So it must have been quite impossible for her to get the nerve up to answer a question or, worse still, to ask one, most especially the BIG one, "May I leave the room?" Consequently she wet her blue flannel bloomers every day about ten o'clock and sat in them, frightened, humiliated, and without hope until her father came with the horse-drawn grain box on runners to transport her through the snowdrifts to whatever warmth awaited at their bleak and failing farmstead.

At least one teacher managed somehow to convey, without using any scatological language, that we were to raise our hand, lifting one finger for "you know what," and two fingers for "the other" when we wished to "leave the room." Just what advantage she derived from the disclosure of our intended bodily function is hard to say, and how she might have detected any discrepancy between the signal and the actual activity remains a mystery. The procedure must have had its roots somewhere in antiquity because the expressions, "doing number one" and "doing number two," were familiar euphemisms for two bodily functions. Yet nobody wrote on the outhouse door, "I paid my nickle and only number threed."

Even without these strange rituals, visiting the school toilet was traumatic enough. As a five year old at Kinley, I'd had to worry about all those suspenders and buttons and garters and not being tall enough, and at Norquay the door was stuck. I don't remember toilets at Frontenac so they must have been the typical outdoor shanties with frost-encrusted seats, unremarkable in their time. But Laura had a tandem biffy with one side for girls and the other for boys. If anyone entered the other side while you were doing whatever number, they could have listened and reported you to the teacher in case you had signalled "number one" when, in fact, it was obvious that you were doing "number two." The boys frequently entered the girls' side and drew anatomically inaccurate illustrations on the walls, and the remaining space on the smooth boards accommodated the entire poetic outpourings of a generation of pubescent bards of both sexes, most of it plagiarized.

The elementary schoolhouse at Laura was a two-roomed affair. Its square shape was divided down the middle by a hallway with a vestibule under the belfry at one end and a big door leading out onto a rather grand wooden stairway with wide balustrades and giving access to a five-acre yard with a playground, four-stall barn, and the tandem biffy at the back. The other end of the hallway had a smaller door letting you out onto a back landing and stairs running down the rear wall.

The classrooms on either side faced in opposite directions so that the side windows sent light in the approved fashion, over the left shoulders of the students. That caused some confusion in geography classes, because the teacher in the west classroom would pull down a map at the front and tell us that east was west, and west was east. But when you graduated to the west room the directions on the map were back to normal. At the front of each classroom there were cloakrooms – east for girls, west for boys.

There were chemical toilets in a cubbyhole at the back of each cloakroom, so in winter, when they were put into use, the boys and girls had a bit more privacy. The pails from these, along with the ashes from the two coal-fired gravity furnaces in the basement, were dumped over the back door banister by the janitor. There was a big, wooden bin on skids there, and once a month or so, the drayman would hook his team of dapple grey Percherons to it and haul it out to the nuisance grounds to be emptied and returned, and neither he nor any of us seemed to have caught anything from it.

Every winter we kids spent recesses pent up in the classrooms for the first few weeks with nothing to do, but finally somebody would start something that would become a craze for a while. One winter it was marbles, another winter mumblety-peg. One spectacular winter started with rocks that struck sparks in the dark, went on to cutting open golf balls and using the long strings of elastic to snap each other in the ass, and ended with cutting open shotgun shells, setting off the caps on the back porch with a rock and a nail, and then putting a match to the powder. Whenever a craze took hold, smoking cigarettes in the barn went way down. But with summer it rose back up to pretty near hundred percent participation among the boys.

There had once been a set of swings in the yard for each sex. They were made of a six-by-six crossbar supported by two upright six-by-sixes sunk into holes lined with concrete. Each crossbar had four eye-bolts with iron rings, from which ropes hung down to make two swings. There was also a double teeter made of three wooden stands with a two-inch pipe threaded through them and a wooden plank teeter pivoted on each side of the center. Eventually the swing posts rotted away and fell over and the teeter planks got carried away for some other use, leaving us with skinning the cat on the pipe as the only alternative to playing tag or softball. Before the swing posts disintegrated one girl was thrown about twenty feet through the air when she pumped up high and the iron ring wore through. So swinging on the remaining three wasn't all that popular any more anyway.

We got a man teacher once who got the bright idea of bringing in his gramophone and a march record. He'd line us up outside like little soldiers, and then he'd turn on his record and march us in to class through the front doors in two lines. But that all ended when we went back to women teachers. They were probably too poor to own gramophones.

It was a woman teacher who sent Bobby Ross home when he got a big, ugly splinter in his bum while sliding down the front steps banister. She was too embarrassed to deal with it herself, although Bobby was willing.

Some time during my elementary schooling at Laura they hooked a bunch of horses onto the old Grain Growers' Hall, where we'd once got our diphtheria shots, and hauled it into the far end of that five-acre school yard. They built a coal shed out back and another tandem privy and that complex of buildings became the new high school. By then the high school population was increasing because drought and depression had pretty well destroyed the job market. Farmers had nothing much to do after they'd shot all their starving horses, so kids were kept on in school. At least it was warm. We learned how to conjugate French verbs (but not to pronounce them); how to parse long, intricate sentences; how to solve simultaneous equations; the names of three or four kinds of triangles; and that if you dissolved a silver half-dollar in nitric acid you could not precipitate it out again as a coin, but only as some bogus-looking metallic powder. All this stuff, as we could have told them, proved to be completely useless after we graduated, but we'd all forgotten it anyway by Christmas, so it never really did us much harm. It probably took a bit longer than that for the kid who dissolved his half-a-buck to forget that chemistry lesson, though.

Character

I last saw Bert Ross, who was blind, in Juniata. Bert had an amazing ability to use his other faculties, and to go with that, he had a great sense of humor. There were a lot of stories about him.

He lived in Kinley, and I think he married one of the schoolteachers there. Bert made his living as a piano tuner, which wasn't a bad trade around 1930 when nearly everyone had a piano in their front parlor and most of the pianos were out of tune. Their tuning soon went out of whack because of the seasonal changes in prairie humidity as well as by the hammering they took from frequent assaults by twelve year olds playing four-handed "Chopsticks."

Bert's wife drove him to his work around the province in their Model T, which was a pretty remarkable thing for a woman to do in those times. One Sunday they had driven over to Juniata to visit mutual friends while we had come over from Laura. When it came time to leave and the car had been started, Bert went out and got into the front seat. But his wife was still yakking away at the door, trying to say all the things she'd had all day to mention but hadn't. So Bert slid over behind the wheel, yelled, "I'm leaving!" and, pushing down the low gear pedal, headed off across the vacant prairie toward the road for home with his wife tearing after him. There was nothing much to run into if he'd kept going, but I guess he loved her because he didn't really let her run very far.

Nearly everybody had a story about bets that he won by doing things that most people would think were next to impossible for a blind man. Like once he walked out of Joe Tate's store, without even his cane, and angled across the street some distance south to the board sidewalk on the opposite side. Then he reached out and put his hand right on the door handle of Jack's Poolroom and walked in.

Another time they said he won a bet on whether he could tell a can of peaches from a can of pears. Some people figured he could sense the right one by feeling the vibrations from the onlookers, but others said he could tell by the way the fruit sloshed around in the cans. The way I figure it, he had a pretty precise map in his head of Kinley and of some of the other places he visited often, and he had a good memory for sounds and the number of steps from place to place. But then, as far as the peaches and pears went, it was a fifty-fifty proposition anyway, so he probably relied a bit on luck as well.

Being a piano tuner, he must have developed a good ear for sounds, and that must have extended over to the sound of voices and the way people put their feet down when they walked. He always knew the local people when he met them, even before they'd opened their mouths. And if there was a stranger around, he knew right away.

After we moved away from Donavon town, my brother Harold had to give up school because there was no grade nine at Frontenac. Grade nine was high school in those days. He used to go into town with Dad to help in the elevator sometimes, and then, after we'd moved to Laura, he left home to start as a trainee with the Royal Bank at Dinsmore. A few years later he was behind the counter in the bank there, when in came Bert with a check somebody had given him for a piano job. The teller at the wicket wasn't too keen on cashing it without identification, but my brother, noticing who it was, spoke up and said he knew Bert and he was alright.

"Why, hello, Harold," Bert called out. "What are you doing away over here?" He'd recognized my brother in a place he could never have expected to find him, and four or five years after he'd last seen him as a fourteen-year-old kid in Kinley.

Another character, I suppose you could call him, was Gramp Rogers, who ran the Saskatchewan Elevator at Laura when we first moved there and who retired, I think, when the Searle company bought it out. He and his wife had come up into Canada from somewhere down in the States, like some of the other Laura people. But so far as I know they were the only ones that drank green tea. I never knew them as anything but "Gramp" and "Grannie," and it seems to me everybody in town called them that without offense either meant or taken. Grannie was of some pretty strict religion and well respected by all, including her real grandchildren as well as the rest of us, and she didn't much approve of her husband's outlandish ways.

Gramp kept a nice, little bay mare in the barn out back of his place. He'd hitch her up to the only one-horse wagon I ever saw to haul rubbish out to the nuisance grounds, or other such chores. When you met him he'd always say, "How's your belly for spots?" And after you got more familiar with him and asked him first, he'd reply, "All healed up and hair growin' on it!" Many parents considered him to be a bad influence, but we kids knew lots of worse stuff than that. It was just a kind of hilarious in-joke between us and him. Later on, when we got older, he told us the one about how to square the circle, but the solution didn't actually seem very funny. I suppose that was partly because our primitive schooling had not broached the fascinating riddles that used to tax the minds of ancient mathematicians. It ran more to working out the time needed by "A" to bail out a cistern with a bucket as compared with the time needed by "B," who emptied a cistern half as big again, using a bucket with twice the capacity, but whose wife interrupted him, once to split kindling and again to put out a fire in the chimney.

Gramp had only one tooth in his head all the time I knew him. It was a big molar in back somewhere, and it must have worn a groove into his opposing jaw because he could close down his gums tight enough to eat just about anything he wanted. One day some of us smart asses were giving him a hard time about that tooth and how old he was and all. We were on our bikes on the sidewalk in front of the Red and White Store, and we'd sort of surrounded him and were leaning over our handlebars and balancing with one foot on the ground and the other leg draped over the crossbars. Somebody said, "Hey, Gramp, I bet you'd like to have a ride on my bicycle, it's a lot more fun than driving that old nag of yours."

I guess Gramp had had enough of the ragging. He pushed the kid so he lost his balance and dropped his bike, and then Gramp picked it up and went riding off down the street lickety-split, clear down to the end, where he turned to cross the railway, and disappeared on the other side of town. He left the bike there, leaning against the front of the poolroom, and went home. The kid who walked two, long, dusty blocks to get back his bike learned another lesson from Gramp that day, probably a more useful one than squaring the circle. Come to think of it, we all did.

There was another character at Laura that everybody knew and respected, but he was a horse. He was the property of the Moncriefs, south of town, and he was a gentle, old buckskin plodder who hauled their democrat or their sleigh the two miles to town and the two miles back seven days a week. Monday to Friday he brought the kids safely to school and safely home, on Saturday somebody would drive him in for groceries, and on Sunday he carried the whole family in to church. The old fellow had two gaits, a slow walk until the driver slapped the reins on his backside and said, "Gitty up, Snap," at which he would break into a slow, shuffling kind of trot.

Many of us town kids had ridden behind old Snap. The Moncrief kids would let us drive because they knew it was impossible for us to do anything that would get his dander up. He wasn't of any recognizable breed and was nothing to look at, but he must have been just about everybody's favorite horse around Laura.

After school one of the boys would lead him out of the school barn and hitch him up, and then he'd drive up to the school to pick up the rest of the Moncrief kids and maybe one or two others who wanted a ride across town. Then, one warm, lazy fall afternoon Snap started out the school yard gate, turned the corner toward the Red and White Store, and quietly dropped dead just in front of the teacherage. Poor old bugger, I thought, poor old Snap.

Somebody phoned the fox farm man, and people got Snap's harness off and pushed the democrat out of the way over in a vacant lot. Then the dray man hooked his team up and drug old Snap off to the edge of town for butchering. There was one little grasshopper of a man that jumped in after they'd got the buckskin hide loose, and he cut open the stomach or something like that, and scooped out a bunch of stuff. He scraped through it and pointed out some little brown bugs. "There ya are," he says. "That's what done it. Bots. Et his stomach all fulla holes."

Well, maybe. I don't know. But I hope not. I hope he just went to sleep. Just got tired and went to sleep.

Institutions of learning

Nobody went on much past grade eight in school, which was called "passing your entrance." Not until the Dirty Thirties, at least, when there wasn't really anything else for kids to do and, anyway, you could hire a good high school principal for forty a month. But although we knew there was a university in the big city where some hoity-toity people carried on the academic farce, we were pretty well certain, wherever we left off our pursuit of scholastic eminence, that we'd learned just about all there was that was worth knowing and a hell of a lot that wasn't.

Like signs of spring. Teachers would always have us bring in signs of winter's end and stand us up in front of the room to brag about our perspicacity. You couldn't blame them I guess, being cooped up all winter between the confines of the dingy schoolhouse and the dilapidated teacherage, with only two recreational outlets: going to the store for groceries and teaching Sunday School to the same smelly, disinterested little urchins they'd faced all week. Signs that June thirtieth might still come, bringing two months of freedom from the little buggers and their piffling concerns, even though it brought two months of no income as well, must have lifted their spirits an inch or two. They didn't seem to realize that most of the signs of spring were fake: stinkweed stays green under the snow all winter; one or two stupid gophers always dig up through frozen ground to spend a day or two in the February

104

sun and then disappear again when the wind swings back to the north; and a few western crows appear in early March and sit around for a month on the bare and frozen poplars fluffing out their black overcoats in a forlorn attempt to insulate the few teaspoons of blood still dribbling around their shrunken carcasses. So when the end of June finally did come the teachers would pack up and leave, fired or fed up or both, and spend the summer writing applications for a job in another town just like Laura or Kinley or Donavon, no better and no worse. What else could they do?

Well, hell, we all knew that the first real signs of spring were high-stepping buggy horses appearing in town one warm Saturday afternoon shorn halfway up their sides with the horse clippers and you knew that all the boys would be coming to school on Monday with bare feet and heads horse-clippered bald and white as mushrooms.

Speech-making. That was another annual pedagogical exercise. Usually the church got in on that too by lending their premises so that we terrified students could be further awed by the carpeted aisles and the altar, the vaulted ceiling, the cold, oak pews full of humiliated parents and judgemental village dignitaries, and by the impossibility that our constricted throats would loosen to project our quavering voices beyond the late comers in the first row. Besides, it was usually shivering cold in the place and our bladders were near bursting.

Instruction consisted of orders to choose a serious topic, write out in our best handwriting enough information about it to occupy five minutes of reading, submit it to the teacher for approval, and then memorize it word perfect. Consequently, our topics were dull, our postures awkward, and our gestures nonexistent. Our self-assurance was destroyed, and our enthusiasm was that of a rooster for the axe. No wonder that we Canadians leave all the talking to politicians and con artists and sit quaking with fear at the thought of rebutting them. Only when we see them on television do we holler some dazzling rebuttal like "Who let you out?" or "Go back to the swamp!"

The big trouble was that our teachers, whether at school or church or at home or in the community, never explained why. Maybe they didn't know why. Why did you put down the seven and carry the three? How come when you put the divisor inside a kind of backwards el-shaped bracket and the dividend in between it and a frontwards el-shaped bracket, and you tried the first figure into the first one or two figures you sometimes got the right figure to write into the empty bracket, and if you didn't, you tried the next bigger, or smaller figure, or something; and then if you didn't make a mistake and you kept on with it, eventually you would have the answer to ninety-seven thousand, six hundred and eighty-four divided by three hundred and forty-seven? And nobody explained why you would want the answer in the first place. And William the Conqueror, 1066. What was the significance of that to us little future citizens of the great big world? Or Magna Carta, King John, Runnymede. "So what?" we wondered. Nobody ever said.

In church they told us not to smoke because it would stunt our growth. But we did, and they did, too, and some of them were big and strong and some of us grew like weeds. One time the preacher had all us boys over to his place for a feed of brown bread and beans and afterwards he told us a story about some young geezer whose girlfriend repulsed his advances so he went to a house where a lot of young ladies lived who were receptive to young men whose girlfriends had turned them away. Later, this young man came down with some unnamed but dreadful disease which wasted him away until, sadly, the poor fellow's spirit departed his body. Most of us boys were too preoccupied by whispering about the likely effect of eating all those beans ("musical fruit," "tooting") to pay much attention to what seemed a pointless story. It wasn't until years later that I realized he had been telling us about some young rapscallion who'd caught the clap and was warning us to stay out of whore houses. Heck, we all knew about that stuff already, but we hadn't the faintest idea where you'd go to find one of those houses.

Demon rum was another lesson. Our Sunday School teacher warned that it would pickle your insides. She brought in a chunk of pig's liver in a sealer of wood alcohol, and she dug it out with a fork to show us how hard and useless it had become from that treatment. Her argument was full of holes. We knew that booze made you drunk and obnoxious and cost a lot of money, and was very likely to get you a punch in the snoot. That seemed like a better argument to us so, naturally, we all suspected there must be more interesting things about booze that nobody wanted to tell us, and maybe it would be worth a little experimentation if we ever got the chance.

I suppose parents tried to teach kids stuff but I don't remember. I can remember learning things taught inadvertently by some of the adults, like how you could strike a kitchen match on the seat of your bib overalls or how you could set a clucky hen on a dozen eggs and hatch out your own flock of Sunday dinners. My parents seem to me to have just taken it for granted I wouldn't become a burglar, a sadist, or a cheat and that they would be satisfied with just about anything else I turned to. Of course most of us showed strong tendencies toward all three callings at one time or another, but generally we just figured we'd grow up and get a job like our dads did or get married, or be a teacher or nurse and then get married, like our mums. You could say, meaning it as a compliment, that most of us had good examples at home and there were plenty more good examples around in the community as well.

But even the practical lessons were confusing sometimes. I watched the local J.P. (justice of the peace), game warden, and kind of town cop break at least three game laws simultaneously one late spring Sunday, when he took his twenty-two rifle and shot a muskrat that had been lured up through a hole in the rotting ice to bask in the warm afternoon sunshine. Could it be so wrong, I wondered, to take gopher tails caught in Harris municipality, where the bounty was three cents, over to the municipal office of Montrose, where they gave you a nickle?

But then maybe practical lessons aren't really lessons at all. Maybe they're just things that happen, like hearing my first dirty story. Was there any gain even though I learned what the Scotsman said to the young lady when his poultry escaped from the crate in his donkey cart? Was there value in coming to understand that although a man was surely a ne'er-do-well if he hadn't got a job of honest work, another man might work honestly for twenty years and be told, "Too bad, we're shutting down your station because it will save us money, so we don't want you any more. Please be out of the company shanty by the end of the month—we're tearing it down to save on taxes"?

And is it a lesson when you hear that the manager of a business has gone into the back and cut his wrists and throat because a letter came in the mail saying the auditor would be there on the morning train? Or that a farmer had come in early from spring plowing a field that the bank had foreclosed and was found, when his wife came to fetch him for dinner, hanging by a halter shank in an empty stall of the big, red barn she'd helped him build?

Is there a lesson in drought and grasshoppers? When people you've grown up with suddenly disappear, taking wives and kids to God knows where, and leaving behind their tools or their furniture or their dog, is that a lesson?

Surely there's a lesson in relief carloads of stuff, shipped clear across the country to help out, that's been gathered up by church congregations and kids bringing cans of food to get into the matinee movie. But it seems like a different lesson when the government ships bales of mouldy alfalfa to feed starving livestock and poisons them instead, or tons of salt fish that nobody has ever seen before and can't eat because they don't know you've got to soak the salt out of it.

It seems to me nobody's really sure just what a lesson is. Can you have a lesson just as long as there was something to be learned, even if everybody missed the point? Or is it only a lesson if the thing that was there to be learned makes an impression on somebody that can be made use of later? I'd say it doesn't much matter. Nobody learns much from lessons anyway. Most of learning comes from being around when something is going on that just happens to interest you.

Risky business

Kids seem to have delighted in risk more than they do now. Our adventures were homemade and consequently full of hidden or unrecognized hazards as well as a few that we knew and ignored.

We were fascinated by fire. Sometimes we would find a railroad fusee when we went walking out the tracks. These were red-paper-wrapped cylinders of flammable chemicals that had a sharp spike in one end. They were dropped onto a wooden railway tie so that the spike penetrated the wood and held them upright, and then the removable cap was taken off, reversed, and scratched across the top of the cylinder much as you strike a safety match on the side of the box. The chemicals thus ignited burned with a fierce, red fire that was a signal to trains that they should stop and find out what danger lay ahead. Sometimes we'd find a whole one that had got dropped accidentally, but usually we got a partly burned fusee that had served its purpose and then been chucked into the snow and extinguished. It was hard to get these used ones going again, but with the application of the heat from half a box of kitchen matches you could usually succeed.

We always saved them until nighttime. It was thrilling to squat in a circle around the menacing stream of fire that shot from a burning fusee. Behind us would be all pitch darkness, but before us, absorbing all our concentration, the red, boiling flame poured out, now and then exploding a spray of the molten stuff at us, threatening to put out eyes and burning neat holes in jackets and pants.

One cold, fall night somebody set fire to the rink and scorched the vestibule and ticket booth before people got it put out. That was the night they were broadcasting Orson Welles's "War of the Worlds" on the radio. There was a lot of talk later about people thinking the Martians really had arrived, but as I remember, they kept cutting in with announcements that it was only a play and not to panic. Anyway, we weren't much interested in science fiction so we didn't stay and listen. Lucky for us we went to another house and played cribbage because when somebody started the rumor that us kids had set the fire we could prove we hadn't been near the rink.

Ammunition was another thing. It was fairly easy to swipe because most people had rifle shells and shotgun ammo around their house or toolshed. One kid dropped a twenty-two shell in the fusee we had burning just to see what would happen and got a piece of the brass casing lodged in the back of his hand when it exploded. We were pretty mad at him because it blew out the fusee and we didn't have any more matches.

We'd pull the bullets out of cartridges with our teeth to get the powder, or if we got hold of a shotgun shell, we'd cut it through in the middle with a jackknife and pour out all the goodies. Then we'd set off the cap with a nail, using a rock for a hammer. The powder was always set fire to eventually, and the lead, especially the shotgun pellets, could be shot at people with rubber band slingshots. I guess most of us must have a high concentration of lead in our body cells since they say it's cumulative. Probably that's why we're all so stupid in our old age. We used to put the pellets in our mouths one at a time and bite them flat between our teeth. There was something enticing about the sensation. It's likely we swallowed the odd one.

We always made a bonfire if we went anywhere, like swimming in the railway ditch or over to the island in the middle of the Big Slough. Often one of the kids would have a paper wrap of powder he'd saved from a shell and carried around in his pants pocket. There were two ways to show off with that. If you dropped the paper pouch right into the middle you'd get an immediate flash of bright, dangerous-looking fire, or you could hold it up high and let it sprinkle down and make sparkles as it reached the heat. Either way made you a hero as long as it lasted.

If nobody was around we'd climb up the ladder inside one of the grain elevators that took you fifty or sixty feet up into the cupola. From there you could look out the windows and see five or six towns across the prairie. You could see people around town doing things they didn't think anybody could see, but they never did anything much except, maybe, go out back to the privy. One time some older kids got up into the top of the Quaker Oats elevator while everybody was in church on Sunday afternoon and then they climbed out through the trap door on the roof and stood astraddle the gable with their arms folded to astound the worshipers strolling home.

Another stunt these older guys started was to wait by the elevators when the evening passenger train pulled in and then they'd jump onto the steps, holding the hand rails, just as she took off. Then they'd ride her a quarter mile or so up the grade where they'd jump off as she picked up speed. One night two of the doors opened and some very strong arms reached out and took a firm hold of two windbreakers, yanking them with their owners right into the coaches. About a mile up the track the boys found themselves chucked out into a snowbank and had to walk ingloriously back into town.

We younger kids were great hunters and trappers. We seldom went out of the house, except to Sunday School, without a homemade slingshot in the back pocket of our bib overalls. And our front pockets were always wearing through from the slingshot rocks we picked out of the railway ballast. Mostly we shot at telephone poles, but if any kind of bird or gopher let us get too close, we were ruthless. Trapping wasn't really dangerous because we mostly trapped gophers for the bounty, but now and again you'd get something else, like a weasel, in your trap and then, look out! A weasel is a real fierce little critter. A weasel will take hold on your finger and hang on like a bulldog.

One summer we got the recipe for making arrow guns. I don't know where it came from, but it very quickly passed, word of mouth, through our gang. It was easy to make one and the materials could be found on pretty near any woodpile and junkheap. You made the barrel of your gun out of two laths. These were plentiful because lath and plaster was the way most houses were finished inside. You bevelled one edge of each and then nailed them together with shingle nails so the sharp edges of the bevels were on the outside. That gave you a V-shaped channel down the middle to lay your arrow into and steer it. Butts were carved out of a piece of two by four and the propellant was a length of inch-wide rubber cut from an old inner tube. The rubber band was attached to the front end of the laths and you then stretched it back and hooked it over the other end. Arrows were carved out of cedar shingles, the thick end forming the point and the thin end cut to a feather shape. Lay your arrow in the groove and use your thumb to push the rubber band loose and that arrow would easily fly a hundred yards. At short range it would go right through a big cabbage and out the other side. Somehow none of us ever shot ourselves or anyone else. I don't know why.

One of the scariest things I remember doing was crawling into a fairly tight-fitting metal culvert under the road so I could be run over by a caterpillar tractor, which was the marvel of the district.

But there was one thing that sure scared the hell out of us, and that included a lot of the grownups. It was Gypsies! Pretty near every summer a half-dozen big cars with straight-eight engines would pull into a vacant lot somewhere and twenty or more Gypsies would come boiling out of them and strike out in all directions. Some would head for the elevators where they knew they'd find a man alone who could be flattered into having his fortune told. Others went into the stores and people said they'd distract the owner while the kids filled up booster bags under their clothes with half the store's merchandise. They'd offer to take the curse off the money in your wallet and some of the pretty girls would tease the bachelors while young boys lifted their wallets. At least that's what people said. But I don't remember anybody being able to prove it.

A lot of mothers ran out and hauled their kids home by the ear so they wouldn't be kidnapped and rustled around to find lost keys to turn the rusty locks of their doors.

After an hour or so we'd hear those big engines start and the Gypsy cars would roar off out the dirt highway and the people would creep out from wherever they'd taken refuge. They'd stand for a minute or so watching the cloud of dust left behind and to make sure the Gypsies weren't turning back for a second assault, and then they'd go visiting back and forth getting and giving the latest embellishment of the disaster.

A nose for news

I was peculiar, I think, because I read the newspapers. Six nights a week the *Star-Phoenix* came out on the train and, as I said, we used to get the Sunday *Chicago Herald* at Donavon. When I was older, some time after we moved to Laura, I discovered *The New York Sunday News*. You could buy that once a week at the barbershop and poolroom and it cost a nickle.

First I read the comics—"Smoky Stover" was the best. It was the Henny Youngman of the comic-strip world, full of one-liners. After you'd read the main story you could look through the panels for ten minutes more, finding little quips and *bon mots* drawn or written in obscure corners. Then there was "Smilin' Jack" flying those fabric airplanes along with his buddy, "Downwind," who never showed his face. "Iggy," "The Little King," and "The Katzenjammer Kids" were there, and "Moon Mullins" and "Kayo." But after the comics, I'd spend hours with each paper reading about all the strange, peculiar, crazy, and disgusting things that went on in America.

Nearly every week there was an account of a lynching. It appalled me. I could never understand how people could take such interest in that degrading activity without doing anything to stop it. And it was quite unbelievable that mobs of ignorant, drunken men—and sometimes women—could storm a jail, remove a prisoner, and kill him in a most barbaric manner, and then go home to neither think nor hear any more about it. Yet these accounts were so frequent that I could only conclude that a lot of people took a definite pride in the practice.

I read about all the gangsters and hoodlums—Al Capone, finally jailed on an income tax evasion rap because nobody could nail him with bootlegging, extortion, or murder; John Dillinger, public enemy number one, gunned down by J. Edgar Hoover's G-men outside a movie theater because his moll ratted on him; Canadian stick-up artist Red Ryan, shot in a bank heist weeks after release from jail as a model prisoner.

There was the long series about the Lindberg kidnapping. In 1927 "Lucky Lindy" (Charles A. Lindberg) was the first to fly solo across the Atlantic, so he was still an almost God-like American hero when six or seven years later, he married Anne Morrow and fathered a baby son. The baby was kidnapped, held for ransom, and finally murdered. There were a lot of fascinating and mysterious clues that engaged the morbid curiosity of readers. There was the ladder found leaning at the nursery window, a Nazi spy connection, ransom notes and ransom money, involvement of high profile Americans and glory-seekers, and finally, Bruno Hauptman, the poor sap who might have owned the ladder, who seemed to have been set up to be the "fall guy" with a few dollars of ransom money, convicted and fried in the electric chair to the delight of broadcaster Walter Winchell and his listeners so that we could all forget about it.

Father Divine's cult was big in New York. You had to admire him. Here he was, a black man living with this white woman, rubbing everybody's noses in it, while extracting millions of dollars, houses, furs, jewelry, and anything else the true believers wanted to put into his greedy hands. The G-men didn't seem to be able to get anything on him, and nobody dared to organize a lynch mob.

I never could decide whether to believe the "human candle" stories. They were common. Usually it was a lady, often a fat lady, who was or was not a smoker, whose remains were found among the coil springs and furniture tacks left when she went up by spontaneous combustion. Sometimes she would have only burnt from the feet up to the midsection, other times from the head down. Then sometimes just an arm or a leg or, best of all, a wooden leg would be left on the floor beside the ashes. Miraculously, the only damage was to the victims and the particular chair they'd been sitting in, but the room was always hung with streamers of oily soot and smudged with smoke stains.

The *Sunday News* always had lots of stuff about boxing: Vancouver's own Jimmy McLarnin and Barney Ross knocking each other silly in alternate victories, James Braddock belting a dray horse to its knees with one punch, and Maxie Baer horsing around with "Da Preem" before punching the poor guy bowlegged. I read Max Schmeling, in *Liberty Magazine,* tell how he would knock out Joe Louis, and then doing it exactly the way he predicted. But then Louis knocked out Schmeling with an illegal kidney punch that everybody cheered because Schmeling was a Nazi, or they said he was. Anyway, it made it okay to cheer for a black man.

From the *Star-Phoenix* sports pages and *The Free Press Prairie Farmer,* I followed the success of Torchy Peden, Canadian six-day bicycle rider; Ethel Catherwood, from Saskatoon, who won the Olympic gold medal in high jump; and the year-after-year world-champion basketballers, the Edmonton Grads. The papers carried pictures and stories of the dirigibles, R-100 and R-101, navigating above the Saint Lawrence River, and then there were the tragic pictures of the Hindenburg explosion and fire, that destroyed it and killed so many people. I followed the hunt for Albert Johnson, the mad trapper of Rat River, and the building of the Bessborough Hotel in Saskatoon. In *The Free Press Prairie Farmer* I always turned first to Arch Dale's cartoon because everybody seemed to hate Prime Minister R. B. Bennett, and Arch had him dead to rights.

One of the kids in Laura used to come around every week selling *The Saturday Evening Post* for a nickle. I used to buy one once in a while if I had another nickle after buying the *Sunday News*. I liked the covers. Everybody now knows about Norman Rockwell's cover pictures, but I always thought they were a bit too cute. Steven Dohanos's covers were better.

There was a magazine called *The Country Guide*. It had a lot of good stuff in it for everybody, but best for me was the weekly page of inventions. They were mostly things invented by farmers, and they used salvaged wheels and gears and inner tubes and haywire and spit. Nearly every week somebody would come up with another ingenious way to close a barbwire fence. They must have published a hundred of them.

We used to get a big roll of overseas editions of the *London Daily Mirror* sent on by cousins in Winnipeg who subscribed to it from England. There was a lot more stuff in them about the rise of Hitler and of Oswald Mosley, the British fascist, than we found in North American papers. I read about Nazi Youth going around smashing up Jewish businesses and forcing their owners to pick up horse dung from the streets with their bare hands, and of *Kristallnacht,* when Nazi mobs rampaged through German streets, burning the synagogues.

There was a kids' page in the *Mirror* with letters, and I wrote one myself advocating a pen pal exchange as a means of combatting warmongering. I got a number of letters – from Britain, Australia, New Zealand, Brazil, and The Gold Coast (now Ghana) – and I kept up a correspondence with most of the writers until I left home in 1938. One of them was a boy named Michael Ventris, an orphan who lived with an aunt in England. He was dead serious about organizing a kids' anti-war club and was well on the way to launching it. He hoped to recruit me as a Canadian liaison, but I think I was too dull for him and the exchange fizzled out. But some years ago I was reading a book about an archaeological expedition, and it had a note on the jacket which mentioned a Michael Ventris, who had become a noted British archaeologist and had died tragically at a young age. I'm sure it was the same person, and I wish I had been more enthusiastic about keeping up our correspondence.

As the 1930s proceeded, there began to be more and more in the papers about depression. Then the dust storms began and I walked home at noon for dinner and returned to school again for the afternoon unable to tell where the sun was in the sky because it was obscured by the dust. In the fall of 1936 I was sitting on the steps of the general store with some of the guys and I happened to look straight up into the sky in the shade of the false-fronted building. Somehow my eyes focused at the right height to see that there was a solid layer of grasshoppers, all moving with the wind and extending without a break in every direction.

Next spring, at Laura, we began to see the first of the dried-out farmers passing through on their way north. Meadow Lake was the Eden they were heading for. The pictures in the papers were now of broken-down cars towing homemade trailers and of Bennett wagons drawn by starving horses, or even by steers no longer worth anything on the market. Barefoot kids were photographed clinging to the ragged dresses of desperate-looking women long past embarrassment of their poverty. And pictures of young men sitting in the open doorways of boxcars or roosted on the catwalks up top were soon followed by others of men rioting at the Saskatoon exhibition grounds and in the streets of Regina.

I would be finishing high school soon. There was nothing to look forward to. My sisters, Connie and Ethel, had gone to Saskatoon as five-dollar-a-month-and-keep housemaids—Thursday afternoons off. My brother Harold was back home, out of a job like all the rest of the youths in town, because the bank let go all their staff who didn't have a high school education. There was no crop, so my dad was lucky to be kept on as caretaker at half-pay—fifty a month. The car was put up on blocks, and the radio battery died, so we couldn't even listen to Amos 'n Andy until the next payday.

"Life is just a bowl of cherries (Don't take it serious)"

It was a fine time to have lived. No, it was glorious. I think it must have been the finest time ever—at least for growing up in that place. You could be ignorant, lazy, stupid, immoral, wasteful, careless . . . It didn't matter. "Time heals all wounds" they used to say. It seemed so.

We lived with a heritage cluttered by baggage carried unwittingly from old, mean, oppressive, and narrow origins. Schools adopted lesson materials that either came directly from these or were copies from them of the kinds of things believed to be good for us. We memorized tables: four gills make a pint (although we never saw a gill); cords of wood at four feet square and eight feet long (treeless Laura would have had trouble finding timber to build even one); rods and chains of land measure; bushels of corn in a crib—ha! better take the baby out first. We had reams in a quire, roods in an acre, drams in an ounce, furlongs per mile, and pounds in a stone. We even tried to learn calculations in pounds, shillings and pence, and sometimes farthings.

There was poetry, too. That was for memorizing. It started almost the first day your mama sent you off to be imprisoned in that dingy, ill-lit, drafty building where you sat all day on a hard, wooden seat with your bum on fire and your knees aching like arthritis because your feet could not reach the floor to relieve the weight pulling on them. The memorizing began with: "The Little Red Hen, she had some chicks.

They said, 'Peep, peep.'" And it went on through "Jack Spratt," "Ding Dong Bell," and all the repetitious stanzas of "The House That Jack Built." In every grade they confronted you with a new *Canadian Reader* full of more stuff to be memorized.

If I remember right, those readers were published in Glasgow. Anyway, they had very little in them that was Canadian. About grade six we began to get a bit of Bliss Carmen and Pauline Johnson, and somewhere in there was stuck Steven Leacock's encounter with the bank. But mostly it was heavy business such as "The Recessional," "Sir Philip Sydney" ("thy need is greater than mine"), "The Moonlight Sonata," and a lot of both poetry and prose on the theme of war and of patriotism for the British Empire in far-flung places. "Breathes there a man with soul so dead," we droned. And once we were released onto the playground we shouted the parody ending: "Who never to his wife has said, 'Get over and give me half the bed.'"

For some reason there remains a vague sense of satisfaction in still being able to recite a lot of those lines, but the most vivid recollections remain for events like the day we came to "The Charge of The Light Brigade." This big farm lad had astounded one and all by stumbling, with not more than a dozen prompts, as far as the line "Not though the soldiers knew someone had blundered." Unfortunately, the unhappy victim had got caught up in the heat of battle so that before he could stop himself "blundered" came out "thundered." The teacher's first impulse was to correct him, but then a snort and a guffaw exploded from her mouth and she fell into an uncontrollable fit of giggling which, after a moment of stunned shock, we all joined with the enthusiasm previously reserved for falling-about-on-the-ground hilarity out behind the barn. It could have been the beginning of a new and better pedagogical relationship, but after recess the poor girl reverted to "Me teacher, you slaves," which was, of course, a safer platform from which to inflict all this upon us.

But that was what you did in school. We all knew that. It wasn't important. Even the function it served in sorting us out according to our supposed mental capacities was limited to the school grounds and, outside the building itself, tended to convey status inversely. Leaders and trend setters in the real world of kids got recognition through their accuracy with slingshots, their access to guns, their possession of smoking material, their stock of dirty stories, or by their skill in some act of physical prowess.

We knew peninsulas and isthmuses, tropics and circles and hemi-spheres, but we knew little of the world even as far as the next town. The rest of the world, we knew, was not all idyllic, but that was only because those other people were not like us. There was nothing wrong with the world. There was nothing wrong with us. It was just those other people. If only they'd . . .

Well, if they didn't, what did we care. Vaguely, we were sure that somewhere along the line we would grow up and get a job or start a farm, and we'd get married and raise families and that's the way it would be. We'd go to the dances and the Christmas concerts, and maybe to church on Sundays. We'd have a car and we'd go to the fair.

There'd be crocuses and buffalo beans and tiger lilies and brown-eyed susans that our kids would bring home to press between the pages of their schoolbooks; we'd pick wild strawberries and saskatoons and chokecherries and pincherries that our wives would put up in quart sealers, and jam and jelly jars, and wine bottles—enough for all winter.

And we'd hunt. Maybe go up north and get a moose. But anyway, there were ducks and geese and sandhill cranes and prairie chickens and Hungarian partridge. Might even go over to the Eagle Hills and get a bear.

We used to say, "You could no more do that than fly to the moon!" There was a joke about a black lady who said, after the plane landed, "The more firma the less terrah." Yes, flying was only for glory-seekers. Some said we'd soon have airmail. Who cared? You could put a three-cent stamp on an order to Eaton's in Winnipeg, put it in the mail for Monday morning's steam train, and a big, brown-paper-wrapped parcel would be in your mail Wednesday night.

It was paradise, and we made the most of it. If we'd been analytical or clairvoyant, or if we'd even been able to see a bit of the world firsthand, we'd have known something was wrong. We'd have been apprehensive, despairing, gloomy, and timid, which would only have spoiled it and accomplished nothing. Perhaps it was good that we were ignorant and provincial. Drought and depression were the only problems we noticed, and they'd probably be over next year. We were sure that in the end we'd be alright, back to normal.

"I wonder what became of Sally?"
(And all the others)

I've been telling all this from my own point of view, which, I guess, is the only point of view a person can have, now that I think about it. Maybe that makes it seem as if I was the only kid around. Well, I wasn't.

But I think my own view of it all is different from most—probably quite at variance on some things. I was more of a loner, so it would be interesting to read the memories of some of the more gregarious survivors of that time and place.

I don't know what ever became of most of the other kids that I encountered, but I'd like to find out. We never imagined there would be a war and that many of us would be soldiers and sailors and airmen, and that some of us would be killed on seas and in lands we had hardly even heard of. We never thought we'd leave the prairie towns and be scattered across Canada, or even to foreign countries. We never imagined ourselves poor or rich or famous, although we all expected some day to be heroic.

Back in the early thirties, when songs like "The Big Rock Candy Mountain" and "Halleluiah, I'm a Bum" were popular, a teacher asked my class what we wanted to be when we grew up. The only exotic occupation I remember hearing came from a kid who lived on a farmstead next to the tracks. He said he wanted to be an engineer. The teacher, wanting to show her sophistication, asked him did he want to be a CIVIL engineer. Not very civilly, he said no, he wanted to be a TRAIN engineer. Teacher wasn't yet ready to get off her high horse so she answered, "My goodness, Lloyd, that's surely a difficult job, steering an engine along the tracks without running it off. You'll really have to concentrate." We all laughed, and Lloyd told her you didn't have to steer the engine, it just followed the rails by itself. He said the engineers were asleep most of the time when they passed his place — that's what he liked about the job. Most of the rest of us said we wanted to be bums. I was one who got my wish.

But before we could begin thinking ourselves grown-up, dust storms, drought, and depression came, and people were struck with panic. Businesses closed their doors and the proprietors disappeared. Farms were foreclosed, the useless machinery was seized by the banks who towed it into town to lie rusting amid the weeds of vacant lots, and the farmers drifted away to God knows where. The youths from the towns went riding the freights, east and west, to look for work that wasn't to be found. Many gave up and took refuge in hobo jungles or in relief camps and dollar-a-day railway maintenance crews. Some of them joined desperate treks and marches and riots and were clubbed and jailed and blacklisted by their government that had said, "Prosperity is just around the corner."

Everything had gone to hell. Desperation gave way to resignation and defeat. Eighty percent of the customers in the Laura general store were living on relief vouchers, and farm produce didn't bring the shipping charges. Honest people learned to cheat to get money to take their kids to the doctor. Church-sponsored relief cars came from the east, and former friends fought over the secondhand clothes in them. And some people in the cities, who still had jobs, hired five-dollar-a-month maids to scrub their floors, wash dishes, do their laundry, iron their linen, make their beds, and carry out the garbage.

Then suddenly the world plunged into the inevitable war that everyone had pretended couldn't happen and everything changed. All was forgiven; crime sheets were wiped clean and blacklists burned. The bums became "Our boys overseas" or "Our BRAVE boys overseas" along with all the rest who went.

Another Lloyd, my seat mate in a double desk through grade eight in Laura, died, a Canadian soldier, somewhere in France. All four of the Macrae boys, quarantined in the big scarlet fever panic, went overseas in air force and army. A grade mate in high school won the DFC flying Lancasters and returned a squadron leader. Another schoolmate, an only son, was shot down and killed. One of the Lester boys joined the army and came home safe, and his brother joined the navy and was killed on convoy patrol in the North Atlantic. Harold and I were both rejected, but Walter, who was nuts about radios and telegraphy, helped build the radio beacons that coordinated D-day, only to come home and die young of liver cancer, a hideous death caused by having spent an afternoon washing a barrack room floor with carbon tetrachloride because some idiot officer was unhappy with the shine on his boots.

One of the Jackson boys from Kinley was killed. Alan and Bill Fowler both got home alright, but I never heard whether Ray Hickman, the boy who recited THAT verse in the teacher's ear, or Jackie Jiggins made it through or not. And Ray Squires was a survivor of the Hong Kong debacle and the subsequent horror of confinement in a Japanese prisoner of war camp.

There must have been many more. Our family's association with Donavon pretty well ended when we moved to Laura except that we went over there once to complete a deal on a secondhand '29 Plymouth, and once, later, I performed there in a play we Laura kids put on. In 1938 I lost contact with the rest of it, except for my parents left at Laura, when I abandoned my five-dollar-a-week job in Dobson's store and hitchhiked and walked east until I ended up in Windsor, Ontario. I spent the war years unheroically, making wheel nuts for army trucks.

Few of us, if any, imagined, let alone foresaw, the changes that put a full stop to that short, deliciously prosaic time before things fell apart. Foreclosed and abandoned homesteads that had once sustained the towns were consolidated into wheat factories by urban-based newcomers. Of the family names I knew, only a few survivors remain in the area today, and fewer, still, continue stubbornly striving to preserve some concept of the halcyon days. Good for you, I say.

You might expect that those of us who left the prairie communities when depression and war ended that naive, uncomplicated era found the sophistication on the outside to be daunting and inhospitable, and that our inferior educations and narrow insights were scorned and ridiculed. Who could have thought that any of us who sat at the feet of the innocent teachers in those primitive prairie shanties, whose most advanced learning aid was a pencil sharpener, would cope?

But many did. A few, I know, went on to be millionaire farmers, and some became businessmen of consequence. There were a number who remained in the armed forces after the war, occupying prestigious commissions and commands. And a lot of us, in the end, did go to universities, some on their own, and many because their war service earned them the opportunity.

As for all the girls, I don't know what became of them. Over the years I'd eventually found quite a few of them interesting, but once I left home, I discovered there were girls in other places too, and lost interest in the ones at home. The war didn't offer much in the way of high adventure for women, but it did open up opportunities outside the range of teacher, nurse, or farmer's wife. In the thirties most girls could only aspire to the first two, but they usually got stuck with the third. Some of them must have seized the opportunity to strike out for glory. I hope so. And I hope they found it.

For all our enthusiasm for sports, I don't think any of us became professional athletes. Some of us can probably brag of playing with or against the Bentley boys from Delisle, or we can at least claim to have watched them. I once saw Max hit a bases-loaded triple off a carelessly thrown pitchout in Saskatoon, when he and Doug were playing hardball in the off season from the Chicago Blackhawks. That's something not many can say.

When I look back, it seems that we were all like baby birds in a colony of down-lined nests, expecting to fledge out and fly about catching bugs and cheeping mindlessly, until one day we put our heads under our wings and fell into a final sleep. But the sand blizzards came, and they ripped the nests away, and we fledglings hopped and fluttered off or crept into shelters amid the debris. A few of us matured there and found forlorn nesting places of our own, but the colonies could not be reconstituted and our own chicks, as soon as their wings could lift them, flew off one by one, hoping to find trees and bugs and gentle rain. And those of us who fled the storms, hopping and fluttering away to alien places, had to learn survival among birds of different feathers, who nested in stark boxes and ate bogus food that gave no clue to its origin. We moulted and refledged in their drab, conformist plumage and learned to squawk and croak and peck each other, and to watch out for the foxes and the kestrels.

Epilogue

When I did all that reading as a kid, there'd often be news items about some old geezer who filled his house up to the roof with junk until he was found dead in the midst of it, or until the authorities came along and hauled it away. It still goes on, and I can understand it.

My house is pretty junky, but most of the junk is books I don't want to part with or intend to read some day, and bits of stuff picked up from places I've been to and been fascinated by. But if I could, and if the authorities would let me, I'd like to have one of Albert Woods's beautiful pony carts parked right in the middle of my front room. And I'd have boxes full of the Imperial Tobacco premium cards they called "Poker Hands," and jars of horehound candy, and a 78 rpm record of "It's Three O'clock in the Morning" and another one of "After The Ball is Over."

I'd have sealers of saskatoons in my cellar and my old pigeons stuffed and mounted in my bedroom. My garden would be full of wolf willows and tiger lilies and buffalo beans. And I'd have a post drill, a leg vise, a trip hammer, and a forge in my garage, and a tire shrinker and a lot of monkey wrenches and tongs. And I'd have a vacant lot with some Shetland ponies, and trees and brush full of songbirds.

And on my front lawn I'd have a dozen or so of those old one-lung, cast-iron engines that used to turn the grain elevators and the grindstones and the water pumps, the ones with the big flywheels and the grease cups and the glass oil reservoirs.

And maybe I'd have a windmill. Oh, and a grain wagon and a cream separator and . . .